WHISPERS FROM THE WRECKAGE

WHERE GOD MEETS YOU IN THE AFTERMATH

PAULETTE BOONE

This book was written from personal experience and reflection. It is offered with the hope that readers will find encouragement, healing, and renewed hope within its pages. Hope often begins as a whisper in the middle of the wreckage.

DEDICATION

To the woman standing in the middle of her own wreckage, wondering if anything can still be rebuilt.

May these pages remind you that your story is not finished, and that even in the ruins, healing can begin again.

ACKNOWLEDGMENTS

Writing this book has been one of the hardest, most humbling experiences of my life. These pages carry pieces of my story, but they are also streamed together with the love, prayers, support, and strength of so many others. I could not have done this without you.

To my Lord and Savior, Jesus Christ. This book exists because You walked with me through the wreckage. When I was broken, You stayed. When I was lost, You guided me. Every word carries traces of Your mercy. Every chapter bears witness to Your grace. You did not leave me where you found me. You wrapped me in Your love and showed me how to live from healing instead of hurt.

To my husband, John. Thank you for your steady strength and unwavering love. You saw me at my lowest and never flinched. When I was unraveling, you stayed anchored and reminded me of who I truly was. You gave me room to wrestle, space to heal, and freedom to write my way through the pain. I am deeply grateful to you. I love you more than words can say.

To my children, Johnathan and Kaitlyn. Thank you for loving me through every season, even the ones I could not explain. Your love never wavered, even when I struggled to see the good in myself. Through you, I learned what unconditional love truly looks like. I am thankful to be your mama, and I love you both with my whole heart.

To my precious grandchildren, Carter, Lakelynn, Remington, and Paisley. Your contagious laughter, your big boone bear hugs, and your joy remind me every day why healing matters. You fill my life with wonder and purpose. You are the heartbeat behind these pages, and your lives are woven into the legacy this story holds.

Lastly, to the friends who showed up when I could barely hold myself together, thank you. Thank you for seeing me when I felt invisible for praying when I had no words. For reminding me, quietly and faithfully, that I was not walking through the wreckage alone. Your presence was a lifeline. Your words were oxygen. You helped me breathe when all I could do was reach for hope. I will never forget how you held space for me when everything felt like it was falling apart.

TABLE OF CONTENTS

INTRODUCTION

There are stories we carry quietly. Stories we live through but never fully talk about. We wrap them in silence, tuck them behind smiles, and keep moving forward as if survival mode was the only option. For a long time, that was me. I did not know how to name my pain, let alone make peace with it. I only knew how to endure. I learned how to keep going, even when everything inside me was breaking.

Maybe you know that kind of silence too. Maybe you have walked through your own wreckage, the kind that left invisible bruises and questions that never found answers. Maybe your wounds were not just physical, but emotional, spiritual, even generational. If so, I want you to know this right from the beginning: you are not alone here.

This book was never about tying things up in a neat bow. Healing is not tidy. It is raw. It is often slow and messy. And somewhere in the middle of it all, I began to hear something I never expected: whispers. Quiet reminders that I was still here. That I had survived for a reason. That the pain I had endured was not the end of my story but a place where something new could begin.

Whispers from the Wreckage is not a collection of polished answers. It is a vulnerable offering of truth, written from the middle of my becoming. It is my story of how I have faced the wreckage of my past, one shattered piece at a time, and discovered that healing does not always look like being put back together. Sometimes it looks like learning how to live whole, even with the scars. Sometimes it looks like holding space for your broken places and still daring to live and dream again.

You will not find perfection in these pages however, what you will find is honesty, grit and grace. You will find a woman who has had to learn how to breathe again, to trust again, to see herself through the eyes of the One who created her and who never left her, even when the pain was too loud to hear His voice.

If you are holding this book, I believe it is for a reason. Not because I have the answers, but because maybe, like me, you are tired of pretending. Tired of carrying the weight of what no one sees. Tired of holding it all together while feeling like everything is quietly unraveling inside. Maybe you are looking for something more than survival. Maybe you are longing to feel again, to hope again, to rise again.

I cannot promise you that healing is easy. It is not. But I promise you this: it is one hundred percent worth it. Every tear, every pause, every moment you choose to stay when it would be easier to numb or run away, every brave yes you whisper into the dark - it all matters. It is all part of your becoming.

This book is tracing the journey of what it means to move from pain to purpose, from wreckage to redemption.

You will walk with me through the shadows, through the process of healing, and into the slow work of becoming the woman I was always meant to be. Along the way, you will find invitational moments for your own reflection, your own healing and I pray you begin to hear your own whispers from the wreckage.

Because this is not just my story. It is a blueprint to help you write your own. So, before we go any further, I want you to pause and take a deep breath. Let it go slowly. You made it here. That is no small feat. Whatever it was that made you pick up this book and to read these pages you are here. And that is where healing begins. Not when everything is perfect, but when we choose to show up fully, in our brokenness and all.

I pray that as you read, you will feel seen. I pray that you will hear the quiet truth that kept me breathing when I could not find the words: there is still hope. There is still healing. There is still a future. And I have found that the most powerful stories rise from the wreckage.

CHAPTER 1

LIFE IN THE SHADOWS

Facing the Reality of a Broken Beginning

There is a kind of pain that swallows you whole. It does not arrive all at once. It creeps in slowly, like a dark cloud settling over your life, until one day you wake up and realize it has covered everything. That is what my life felt like. One long, unending night.

There were certain sounds that changed everything. The click of a door closing. The quiet that followed. The subtle shift that only I seemed to notice. Most people would not have thought twice about it. But my body did.

I did not need an explanation. I had learned what that kind of quiet meant for me. My heart would begin to race before anything unfolded. Not because something had already happened, but because I understood the pattern. The anticipation was suffocating. It filled the room long before anyone else felt it.

I would sit in my room waiting, listening to the silence grow heavier. I remember wishing time would stand still in those moments. If it could just pause, maybe I could stay suspended in the before. But time never paused. It always seemed to speed up when I wanted it to freeze and then slow down when I needed it to pass.

So, I prepared myself. Stay strong. Do not cry. Whatever you do, do not cry. I believed that emotion had consequences. I believed that tears could make things worse. So, I swallowed them before they formed. I steadied my breathing. I stayed still.

Some children learn to relax when a house grows quiet. I learned to brace. And that was the beginning of the shadows. I did not understand it at the time. I only knew how to brace. I only knew how to quiet myself before I could be quieted. I did not realize that moment was teaching me something I would carry for years.

It was teaching me that strength meant silence. That safety meant shrinking. That emotions were liabilities. I did not know I was stepping into survival. I only knew I wanted it to stop. And the shadows felt safer than being seen.

I cannot pinpoint the exact moment hope slipped away. But even then, beneath the wreckage, there were whispers. Gentle truths trying to reach me through the silence. I could not hear them yet, but they were there.

You may be holding this book because you are tired of being strong. Or because you have survived things you never talk about out loud. Maybe you are not sure why this story found you, only that something inside you recognized it.

If that is you, I want you to know this from the very beginning. You are not broken for still hurting. You are not weak for needing more time. And you are not alone in what you carry.

This story is not here to rush you toward healing or ask you to be brave before you are ready. It is here to sit with you. To name what has been buried. To make room for the parts of you that learned to survive quietly. There is no finish line you need to reach as you read these pages. There is only permission to be honest about where you are.

It was never just one thing. It was years of hurt layered on top of one another. Emotions that were silenced again and again. Trauma that left wounds far deeper than anyone could see. Battles I fought quietly within myself. I learned how to live inside pain, carrying it like a reflex that slowly became my identity.

It kept me alive, but it came at a cost. It taught me how to endure, not how to rest. It trained my body to stay alert and my heart to stay guarded. Even in moments that should have felt safe, I remained braced, waiting for something to go wrong. I did not know how to stand down from that posture. I only knew how to keep going.

Over time, I began to believe that holding everything together was the same as being strong. I believed that if I could just hold everything together long enough, the pain would eventually lose its voice. But pain does not disappear when it is ignored. It settles deeper. It finds new ways to speak. And eventually, it begs to be acknowledged.

The Weight of the Past

Growing up, I learned how to endure, but not how to heal. Pain became familiar and hiding it became second nature. I smiled when I needed to. I held everything together because falling apart did not feel like an option.

Inside, I was breaking. I became skilled at pretending. I knew how to put on a brave face, how to nod and agree, how to steer conversations away from anything that might expose what I was really carrying. If I stayed busy, if I kept performing, maybe no one would notice the cracks beneath the surface.

I learned early that my emotions were seen as excessive; that feeling deeply made me a problem instead of a person. Vulnerability was met with dismissal rather than care. So, I buried everything, pressing my pain so far down that I eventually lost sight of where it began.

The trauma of abuse did not just wound my heart. It reached into my sense of identity. It shaped how I saw myself, how I moved through the world, and how I measured my worth. I grew up believing lies about who I was. That I was unworthy. That I was not enough. That I was broken beyond repair.

Those lies became the voice in my head. They whispered to me daily, reminding me that no matter what I did, I would never be good enough or whole.

And as I got older, that brokenness did not disappear. It simply took on new forms.

I carried it into friendships, constantly afraid of being too much or not enough. At times, I swung to the opposite extreme, clinging too tightly, asking more of others than they were able or willing to give. I carried it into relationships, allowing myself to be treated in ways that confirmed the lies I already believed. I carried it into motherhood, terrified that my pain would somehow spill over onto my children.

No matter how hard I tried to outrun it, my past followed me, whispering that healing was not meant for someone like me.

I learned how to function while always bracing for impact, but there were more days than not when even functioning felt impossible. Getting out of bed took everything I had. I carried exhaustion, fear, and an aching loneliness that came from pretending to be okay when I was anything but. That fear kept me locked in a cycle I did not know how to escape.

Silent Battles and Hidden Pain

Abuse teaches you how to live on constant alert. It rewires your instincts and trains your body to respond with restraint instead of trust. I learned how to anticipate moods, how to read a room before I ever stepped into it, how to stay quiet when the atmosphere shifted.

I could sense tension before a word was spoken. I became aware of every look, every sigh, every sudden silence. My world depended on keeping the peace, even if it meant silencing my own voice.

What I did not realize at the time was that I was building my life around fear. Fear of what might happen if I said too much. Fear of what vulnerability could cost me. Fear that if I needed too much, I would be punished, rejected, or left.

So, I adapted. I adjusted. I abandoned my own emotions to make room for everyone else's comfort. I smiled when I was expected to. I stayed small when everything inside me wanted to scream. I learned how to be agreeable, even when my soul was begging for more.

For a long time, this felt normal. I did not realize how abnormal it truly was. What happens when survival mode becomes your default? When the very tools that once helped you survive begin to steal the life you were meant to live? That question followed me for years.

I carried the weight of my past into every space. Every conversation. Every relationship. It clung to me like a shadow. It shaped how I responded to love and how I interpreted silence. I second-guessed everything I said. I replayed conversations, wondering if I had said too much, asked for too much, or made others uncomfortable.

Even in moments of laughter, there was hesitation in my chest. A quiet warning that said, do not get too comfortable, this will not last. I could be surrounded by people who cared about me and still feel completely alone.

Life was happening around me, but I felt separate from it. Disconnected from the very moments I longed to belong to. Proverbs 14:13 says, "Even in laughter the heart may ache, and the end of joy may be grief." That verse described me perfectly. I had grown so used to masking pain that joy felt foreign, like something I could observe but not fully receive.

People filled the space around me, but loneliness filled the space within me. Not the kind that comes from being physically alone, but the kind that lingers even in the presence of others. A deep soul emptiness that no amount of social connection could touch.

I had built walls around my heart so high and so thick that I forgot what life looked like on the other side. I believed I was protecting myself. I told myself I was keeping pain out. But what I did not realize was that while I was guarding against hurt, I was also shutting out love.

I longed to be fully seen and accepted. I wanted someone to look at all of me and stay. Yet I was terrified of being exposed. Terrified of what someone might do with my truth. So I kept my distance. I shut the doors. And still, I found myself quietly hoping someone would knock hard enough to be let in.

The isolation was subtle. On the surface, I was social. I could listen, empathize, and offer advice. But underneath, my heart was guarded. My trust was fractured. Every time I wanted to reach out, something inside me froze. A voice whispered, do not bother. They will not understand. You are too much. You are not enough.

So, I stayed silent. I carried it alone. And the loneliness deepened. I began to understand that living on guard does not end when abuse ends. It lingers. It becomes a lens through which you see the world. I struggled to believe I could be loved without earning it. I struggled to believe I could be cared for without performing.

That struggle showed up in quiet ways. I shrank myself in conversations. I said yes when I wanted to say no. I minimized my emotions and dismissed my pain so I would not appear demanding. I lived in constant fear of rejection, even in spaces meant to be safe.

And the hardest truth of all was this, in trying so desperately to keep the peace, I was rejecting myself.

The peace I thought I was protecting was fragile and false, built on silence and self-neglect. It was the kind of peace that eventually shatters.

There came a moment when I could no longer ignore what I was doing. I had to name the loneliness. I had to confront the lies. I had to admit how deeply I was hurting. Not for attention. Not for sympathy. But for freedom. Because healing cannot happen in hiding. And I was so very tired of hiding.

What I did not know then was that surviving had already required courage. I had spent years believing I was weak because I was tired, because I struggled, because I had not moved on. But the truth is, it takes immense strength to endure what you were never meant to carry alone. The fact that I was still standing, even in the shadows, was not evidence of failure. It was evidence of resilience.

Healing would come later, slowly and imperfectly. But before healing could begin, I had to tell the truth about how heavy survival had been. I had to stop minimizing my pain and start honoring what it took for me to make it this far.

When the Body Breaks Too

By the time I reached adulthood, the emotional wounds I carried had begun to show up in my body. What I could not release internally began demanding attention physically. I was diagnosed with clinical depression and bipolar disorder, my emotions swinging between extremes that left me exhausted and disoriented.

Some days I felt numb, disconnected from everything and everyone around me. Other days, despair pressed so heavily on my chest that even the smallest tasks felt impossible. Getting out of bed. Brushing my hair. Speaking. It was as if I were trapped inside a body that refused to move and a mind that refused to hope.

Then came the migraines. Then fibromyalgia. The pain was not occasional. It was constant. An ache that lived deep in my bones. A fatigue that no amount of sleep could touch. I woke up tired, spent my days hurting, and went to bed knowing tomorrow would likely feel the same. It felt like my body had turned against me, as though it was carrying the weight of everything I had endured for far too long.

I was drowning. The physical pain fed the emotional turmoil, and the emotional turmoil intensified the physical pain. It was a cycle I did not know how to interrupt. Slowly, I began disappearing from my own life. I was present, but not really there. Existing, but not living.

I wanted to be a good wife. I wanted to be the kind of mother my children needed and deserved. I longed to be engaged, attentive, and fully present. But most days, I felt invisible in my own home, watching life move forward while I remained stuck in the shadows.

I would sit quietly, observing my family, convinced I was failing them. I wanted to tell them how much I loved them, how much I wished I could be more. But the words stayed trapped inside me. Instead, I swallowed my pain and told myself they deserved someone stronger. Someone healthier. Someone less broken.

Someone who was not me.

I did not know how things would change. But slowly, gently, I was learning how to breathe again.

And in that breath, healing began to find its way in.

Listening from the Wreckage

There comes a point when silence stops being empty and starts becoming an invitation. It becomes the space where something deeper begins to stir. That space is rarely comfortable. It is messy. Tender. Unsettling.

That is where the wreckage begins to speak.

For me, it happened in the stillness of my lowest moments. When I had nothing left to give. When survival no longer felt sustainable. In that quiet, I began to hear something gentle rising from everything I had buried. A whisper that came without judgment. A reminder that even though everything felt broken, something within me was still alive.

I had spent years outrunning my pain. Years pretending, I was fine. Years holding myself together out of fear that if I stopped, everything would fall apart. But it was in the unraveling that I finally began to feel. In the undoing, I started to see myself clearly. Not as someone who had failed, but as someone who had survived more than anyone knew.

And it was there, in that place, that I met God again.

He was not waiting for me on the other side of healing. He was sitting with me in the wreckage. He was not asking me to fix myself. He was asking me to be honest. He reminded me, gently and steadily, that His presence was not dependent on my strength. It was anchored in His love.

The wreckage did not scare Him. The silence did not offend Him. My sorrow did not disqualify me. He drew closer, not further away. And when I allowed myself to feel it, when I allowed myself to name what hurt, I realized something surprising.

I was not just falling apart.

I was making room.

This chapter does not end with resolution. It ends with breath. With honesty. With an invitation to stay present in the middle of your own wreckage and listen to the whispers rising within you. The ones that do not demand performance, only permission.

If you are still there, still sitting in the ache, hear this. You are not alone. And you are not beyond hope. Even now, something tender is stirring. Not in spite of your brokenness, but right in the middle of it.

Your wreckage may feel loud. But the whisper is louder. And it speaks through mercy.

You are still here. And that matters. I did not know it then, but the shadow was not just around me. It had begun to live inside me. It shaped the way I saw myself. It shaped the way I saw God. It shaped the way I believed love worked.

And when you live in the shadows long enough, you forget there was ever light.

CHAPTER 2
WHISPER OF HOPE IN THE DARKNESS

Crying Out in Desperation

I did not know that a single year could hold so much grief. I did not know how quietly loss could weave itself into everyday life, settling in without warning and dismantling what once felt steady. That year did not arrive with catastrophe or spectacle. It came disguised as responsibility, adjustment, and endurance.

And before I understood what was happening, the carefully constructed life I had built began to crack under the weight. At first, nothing looked different from the outside. I was still functioning. Still showing up. Still carrying what needed to be carried. From a distance, I looked steady. Capable. Strong.

But strength had begun to feel heavier. The responsibilities that once felt purposeful began to feel relentless. The expectations I had managed for years began to press harder against my chest. I told myself it was just a season. Just a stretch. Just something to get through.

But the stretch did not ease. The fatigue settled in quietly. Not the kind that sleep fixes, but the kind that lingers in your bones. The kind that follows you into every room. I would wake up already tired. Already bracing. Already calculating how much of myself I could afford to give that day.

Relationships began to feel strained in ways I could not easily explain. Conversations required more effort. Smiling felt intentional instead of natural. I was present, but not fully there. And somewhere beneath all of it, something deeper began to shift.

I had spent years building a version of myself that could handle anything. The dependable one. The steady one. The strong one. But as everything around me grew heavier, I began to wonder who I was without that strength.

And that question frightened me more than the exhaustion. I kept telling myself I could manage it. That if I just tried a little harder, organized a little better, prayed a little longer, I could steady what felt unstable. I tightened my grip instead of loosening it. I pressed forward instead of pausing. But there is only so long a person can carry weight without setting it down. And eventually, my body made the decision my mind refused to make.

That season exposed how thin my strength had become. I was no longer just tired. I was unraveling from the inside out, and I did not know how to stop it. That unraveling did not stay contained inside my thoughts. It began spilling into the practical, everyday places of my life, places where I no longer had the margin to compensate or recover.

When my work schedule shifted from part time to full time, I told myself I could handle it. I always had before. I believed I would adjust, find balance, and push through. But working nights did more than disrupt my sleep. It disrupted my sense of grounding. My internal rhythm disappeared, and with it, the routines that once helped me feel anchored. What I lost was not only rest, but connection.

I missed sitting down to dinner with my husband. I missed the quiet togetherness that had once held us steady at the end of the day. Our lives began passing each other instead of intertwining. I felt like a guest in my own home, moving through familiar spaces that no longer felt safe beneath my feet. Life continued happening around me, but I felt removed from it, as though I were watching everything through a pane of glass.

My body stayed exhausted no matter how much I slept. My heart felt disoriented, unsure of what it needed or where it belonged. And just as I was beginning to accept one layer of loss, my body introduced another. The diagnosis of Celiac disease changed everything.

Suddenly, food was no longer simple. Every meal became a source of anxiety. Every invitation to eat required explanation, planning, and vigilance I did not have the energy to maintain. I read labels obsessively, questioned ingredients, and rehearsed conversations before ordering anything. What once nourished me now reminded me constantly of what I had lost.

I began to feel like a burden. An inconvenience. Even to myself. I resented how complicated my body had become, how fragile everything felt. It was as if my body had turned against me, exposing limits I did not know how to accept. I no longer felt safe inside myself. The loss of safety within my own body quietly eroded the little stability I had left.

The emotional toll was heavier than I expected. I was not simply overwhelmed. I was undone.

I struggled to focus at work. I was distracted at home. I neglected my own needs without realizing how deeply I was disappearing. Everywhere I looked, I felt as though I was falling short. My thoughts raced endlessly, trying to fix everything at once, while my body remained too exhausted to follow through on any of it.

I was anxious. I was angry. I was worn down in ways I did not know how to name.

And still, I pretended.

I smiled when people asked how I was doing. I showed up because it felt like the only option. I reminded myself that others had it worse and that gratitude should be enough to carry me through. I convinced myself that falling apart was not allowed, that strength meant silence. But the truth was, I was already falling.

Quietly.

Invisibly.

And no one could see how heavy the weight had become.

Fear stepped in where control had once lived.

It crept into everything. I began waking up with a tightness in my chest, a sense of dread I could not explain. I would lie in bed before work, staring at the ceiling, struggling to breathe through the panic that met me before my feet ever touched the floor. I questioned myself constantly. Was I losing control? Was I slipping back into a darkness I had fought so hard to escape.

Depression did not announce its return. It simply settled in as though it had never left.

Anxiety followed closely behind, shrinking my world until even the smallest tasks felt overwhelming. Each day required more effort than the last. Each step forward felt uncertain. I did not know how to ask for help without feeling ashamed. To admit I was drowning felt like admitting failure.

Silence felt safer than being misunderstood.

So I stayed silent.

I told myself rest would fix it. I told myself it would pass. I told myself that if I pushed a little harder, things would improve. But pushing was no longer working. The ground beneath me was giving way, and I was out of energy pretending I could hold everything together.

A Cry from the Floor

What had been building quietly for months finally reached its limit. It did not arrive with drama or noise. It came on an ordinary afternoon as I prepared for another long night at work. The house was still. Everything looked normal. But inside me, something gave way. I had felt the tears pressing behind my eyes all day, waiting for permission to fall. And finally, I stopped fighting them.

I collapsed onto the living room floor. My knees hit the carpet as the weight of everything I had been carrying rushed through me all at once. The tears were not gentle.

They were raw and unrestrained, rising from a place deeper than I knew existed. I cried until my body ached, until my voice grew hoarse, until my hands shook and my face was soaked.

I was not simply sad.

I was desperate.

And in that desperation, I prayed.

It was not a polished prayer. It was not articulate or composed. It was the kind of prayer that rises when there is nothing left to hold back. I did not have strength to perform faith that day. I did not have words that sounded spiritual. I only had exhaustion.

I remember whispering, "I cannot keep doing this." Not with anger. Not with accusation. Just with emptiness. I had nothing left to prove. Nothing left to manage. Nothing left to hold together.

For the first time in a long time, I was not bracing.

I was surrendered.

I was not asking for everything to be fixed. I was not asking for rescue or relief. I only needed reassurance. I needed to know I was still seen. Still held. Still heard. I did not know then that reassurance would come so gently.

A Whisper in the Darkness

After the sobs slowed and my body grew still, silence settled in. Not a peaceful silence, but a fragile one. The kind that follows a storm and leaves you unsure of what will come next.

I remained there on the floor, my cheek pressed against the carpet, my spirit emptied. Nothing around me had changed. My circumstances were the same. The pain was still present. And yet, something in the room felt different.

It was subtle. Delicate. Like the faintest shift before night begins to lift.

I tried to pray again, but no words came. Doubt crept in. I wondered if I had cried too late or too often. I wondered if God was tired of my questions.

And then, without sound or spectacle, something settled deep within me. Not a thought, but a knowing.

Paulette, your pain is not in vain. Your pain will become the platform you will stand on to fulfill your purpose.

The words carried weight and peace at the same time. I knew they were not my own. God had answered me, not with thunder or fire, but with a whisper.

Tears filled my eyes again, but these were different. Quiet. Sacred. I had asked for something to hold onto, and He had given me meaning.

Not escape.

Not instant relief.

Meaning.

I did not understand how pain like mine could ever be used for good. I did not know how something so heavy could become anything beautiful. But I trusted the One who spoke. Because He met me there on the floor, when I felt least worthy of pursuit.

And while nothing around me changed, everything within me began to shift.

Learning to Take the Next Step

That moment did not erase my pain or resolve my circumstances. My body still hurt. My schedule remained chaotic. Fear still whispered. But I was no longer reaching for answers. I was learning how to rest in His presence.

Hope did not arrive loudly. It arrived steadily and near. For the first time in a long while, I did not feel abandoned in my suffering. I felt accompanied.

That whisper became a lifeline. I returned to it again and again in the days that followed. When anxiety rose. When old lies resurfaced. When exhaustion threatened to pull me under. God did not rush me. He did not shame me. He met me exactly where I was and reminded me that His presence was not distant from my pain. It was woven into it.

When everything else is stripped away, when the darkness feels endless and the noise fades, God still speaks. Sometimes, all it takes to begin again is a whisper in the middle of the wreckage.

This was not the end of my story. It was the moment hope found its way back in.

For the first time, I understood that survival had carried me this far, but it would not carry me where I was being led next.

CHAPTER 3

EMBRACING BROKENNESS

The Tender Reality of Brokenness

There is a tender place that only reveals itself once we stop striving to be okay. It is not the kind of place we stumble into casually. It is the result of long nights filled with tears that no one sees, mornings where it takes every ounce of strength just to get up, and days when pretending feels like the only way to survive. This space is not clean or comfortable.

It is raw.

It is fragile.

And yet, it is holy. It is where truth begins to rise through the silence, and where the presence of God meets us with compassion rather than judgment.

There were seasons when I did not know how to admit I was not okay. I could smile, answer questions, and keep moving, but inside I felt brittle. My body carried tension like it was normal. My mind stayed busy trying to manage what my heart could not say out loud. Even in quiet moments, I felt on edge, as though peace was something meant for other people. And when I finally stopped striving long enough to feel what was true, it was not pretty. It was not organized. It was a collapse I could not control, and yet it was also the first moment I realized God was not repelled by my mess. He was near.

To embrace brokenness is to accept that there is no shortcut through the pain. It is realizing that healing does not begin when everything is fixed; it begins the moment we admit that we are not. There is something painfully beautiful about looking at your life and acknowledging what has been lost, what has been shattered, and what still aches. It is a form of honesty that costs something, but it also gives something in return. It offers freedom of no longer needing to hide.

Many people confuse brokenness with failure, but that is a lie the world tells to keep us striving for an image of perfection that no one can sustain. Brokenness is not failure. It is the evidence that you have lived, that you have loved, that you have tried, and that life has touched you in real and sometimes devastating ways. There is no shame in it. In fact, there is dignity in choosing to face it rather than running from it.

When we allow ourselves to feel the depth of our brokenness, we are also allowing ourselves to begin healing. It is not a fast process. It does not follow a schedule or offer easy answers. But it does begin to soften the rough edges we have built around our hearts. It creates room for compassion, truth and grace. And slowly, without even realizing it, we start to loosen our grip on what we thought we had to be to be worthy.

You do not have to prove yourself to God. He already knows. He has seen the moments when your strength gave out. He has heard the prayers you didn't have words for. He has stood with you in the quiet and waited patiently for the day you would give yourself permission to come undone in His presence. You do not have to perform for healing. You only need to be willing to show up. And even if you show up broken, even if all you can bring is the weight of your sorrow, that is enough. Because brokenness in the hands of God is never wasted.

The tender reality of brokenness is this: it strips away what is false and reveals what is true. You were never meant to carry it all. You were never meant to be the one holding everything together while your soul crumbled beneath the pressure. God is not asking for your perfection. He is asking for your permission to enter places where it hurts and begin to bring healing from the inside out.

In this tender space, where truth and pain collide, something powerful happens. You begin to see yourself not as someone who is beyond repair, but as someone deeply worthy of restoration. You begin to trust that maybe, just maybe, God can take the pieces and make something beautiful again. And you begin to believe that healing is not just possible, it is already beginning.

And once that truth begins to rise, the next step is not to rush yourself into being better. The next step is to open the places you have kept guarded and let God meet you there, not in the version of you that has it together, but in the places where you are still cracking.

Letting God into the Cracks

We spend our lives learning how to hide what hurts. It begins subtly, often in childhood, when we are told to stop crying or to be strong. I am sure we have all heard and maybe even said ourselves, "If you don't stop crying, I'll give you something to cry about." We internalize the idea that pain is something to be concealed, not something to be welcomed or honored. So, we learn to cover the cracks. We learn to smile when our hearts are heavy, to show up when we feel empty, to say we are fine when we are breaking inside. And the longer we do this, the easier it becomes to believe that the only way to be loved is to remain put together.

But healing does not happen in the places we hide. Healing happens in the cracks, in the broken spaces where our need is too great to be ignored, and our strength has run out. These are the places God waits for us to invite Him in with a simple whisper: I cannot carry this alone anymore.

If that feels too big, start smaller. You do not have to hand God every painful detail in one breath. Sometimes the bravest prayer is simply, I am here, and I do not know what to do with this. Sometimes it is letting yourself cry without apologizing.

Sometimes it is admitting you are tired of being strong.

God does not require a perfect confession. He responds to honesty. One crack at a time is still an opening, and even the smallest opening is enough for light to begin entering.

Letting God into the cracks means acknowledging that there are parts of our stories we would rather avoid. There are memories we have buried deep because they feel too heavy to face. There are wounds we have covered for so long that we forgot they were still bleeding. And yet, God already knows. He has seen every moment of pain. He has witnessed every time you held your breath just to make it through the day. He has watched the tears that fell behind closed doors and heard the thoughts you were too afraid to speak aloud.

He is a gentleman who will never force His way in. He waits for the invitation. And when you extend it, even trembling and unsure, He steps gently into the mess. He does not flinch at the sight of your pain. He does not turn away in disappointment. He kneels in the wreckage with you and begins to rebuild not in haste, but with care.

When we let God into the cracks, we stop pretending that strength means doing everything on our own. We stop believing the lie that vulnerability is weakness. We begin to understand that true strength is found in surrender. It is found in the moment we stop patching ourselves up with temporary fixes and instead lay the shattered pieces at the feet of the One who knows how to make all things new.

God does not enter with condemnation. He enters with compassion. He does not shame us for being broken. He honors the courage it took to open the door. He holds every piece and whispers truth over what has been twisted by pain. He replaces lies with truth. He replaces fear with faith, and He replaces despair with hope.

This is not a one-time act. Letting God into the cracks is a daily choice. It is waking up each morning and choosing to be honest about where you are still hurting. It is allowing yourself to be seen in your most vulnerable places and trusting that God will meet you there again and again. Some days that will feel scary or uncertain. Other days it will feel like a relief. But no matter what it feels like, it is sacred.

Healing does not require you to be whole first. It requires you to be open. Open to the possibility that what feels ruined can be restored. Open to the truth that you do not have to do this alone. Willing to accept the kind of love that sees you at your worst and calls you worthy anyway.

There is beauty in the cracks. Not because they are pretty or polished, but because they are honest. They tell the truth about what you have survived. They speak of battles fought in silence, of strength that no one could see, of resilience that cannot be measured. And when you allow God into those cracks, you are allowing His light to shine through them.

The cracks are not the end of your story. They are the beginning of something beautiful. They are the invitation to be fully seen, fully known, and fully loved. And they are the place where the healing of God begins to pour in, not to erase the pain, but to redeem it.

And when you have lived in those cracks long enough, something else begins to happen. Pain stops being only something you carry and starts becoming something that names you.

It shapes the way you see yourself, the way you interpret love, and the way you decide what you deserve. That is why healing is not only about feeling better. It is also about reclaiming who you are.

Recognizing How Brokenness Shapes Identity

Pain has a voice, even when we do not speak. It has a way of slipping into our thoughts, rewriting our memories, and reshaping the way we see ourselves. It begins subtly, whispering that we are not enough, that we are too much, or that we are somehow the reason everything fell apart. And if we are not careful, those whispers turn into beliefs.

For many of us, brokenness did not just hurt, it started to define us. This is where many of us begin living from sentences we never chose.

I am too much.

I am not enough.

I am hard to love.

I am always the one who ruins things. I have to earn my place. I have to stay quiet to stay safe. Those thoughts can feel like truth because they have been repeated so many times, by others or by our own wounded minds. But they are not the truth. They are survival languages. And God does not speak to you in survival language. He speaks to you as His beloved.

We began to see ourselves through the lens of what happened to us rather than who we really are. We were not just abandoned, we became unlovable. We were not just rejected, we became unworthy. We were not just silenced, we became invisible. The pain that was caused to us became the filter through which we viewed our new identity.

Recognizing how brokenness has shaped your identity is one of the bravest parts of healing. It requires you to look at the places where your sense of self was twisted by trauma and gently begin to untangle the lies from the truth. It is not about pretending the pain does not exist. It is about reclaiming your identity from the wreckage of what tried to steal it.

You were someone before the breaking. Before the abuse. Before the heartbreak. Before the betrayal. Before the diagnosis. There was a version of you, innocent, tender, full of dreams and who still exists beneath the fragments of what life tried to bury you under. And even though you may feel far from her, even though time and pain have changed you, that core of who you are is still alive.

God did not create you with fear as your foundation. He did not design you with shame written into your bones. He did not speak you into existence only to have the world convince you that your worth depends on your performance, appearance, or ability to hold it all together. He created and formed you in love. He called you good. And that original design is not lost. It is simply waiting to be uncovered again.

When you begin to see how brokenness shaped your identity, you will also begin to see how it skewed your vision. It kept you small. It kept you silent. It kept you from dreaming. But you are allowed to want more. You are allowed to reach for joy, even if you are still healing. You are allowed to rewrite the story you were handed and name yourself with the truth of who you were always meant to be.

This process is not about blame. It is about awareness. It is about gently and honestly naming the moments that made you question your worth and choosing to see them in the light of grace. It is about looking at your story and saying,

"Yes, that happened to me. But it is not the whole of me." Your pain is a chapter, not the entire book. Your wounds are real, but they are not your identity.

Rebuilding identity from a place of brokenness takes time. It takes kindness. It takes consistent truth-telling, even when the lies sound louder. Some days you will feel like you are making progress. Other days you will feel like you have taken three steps forward and two steps back. That is part of it. That is what healing looks like. It is not a straight path. It is a messy unraveling that leads to deeper truth.

And in this process, God meets you. He reminds you of who you are: chosen, seen, cherished, and redeemed. He whispers your name back to you when you have forgotten it. He speaks life into the places where pain tried to define you. And He does not rush you. He walks with you. Step by step. Layer by layer. Truth by truth.

As you recognize how brokenness shaped your identity, you also open the door for healing to reshape it. You begin to let go of false narratives. You stop striving to be someone you were never meant to be. You come home to yourself not shaped by shame but shaped by grace. And in doing so, you give yourself permission to live with a new kind of freedom. A freedom rooted not in having it all together, but in knowing you are loved exactly as you are.

When brokenness shapes identity, shame often becomes the voice that keeps it in place. Shame keeps you rehearsing the old story. It keeps you hiding the parts of you that still hurt. It convinces you that if people saw the real you, they would leave. That is why healing is not complete until shame is confronted, because shame does not only affect how you feel. It affects how you live.

Moving from Shame to Self-Acceptance

Shame is a silent intruder. It does not burst through the door with noise and chaos. Instead, it tiptoes in, quiet and unnoticed, until it finds a home in the corners of your soul. It does not only speak harsh words; often, it whispers in subtle tones that sound familiar. Shame does not just tell you that you did something wrong. It tries to convince you that you are damaged.

For me, shame was not always loud. Sometimes it sounded like caution. Do not say that. Do not ask for that. Do not show that part of you. It trained me to second guess myself, to shrink my needs, and to measure my worth by how well I could keep things together. Even on days when I looked fine on the outside, shame still had a way of making me feel exposed on the inside. It made love feel risky. It made rest feel undeserved. It made tenderness feel like something I had to earn.

For some, shame comes from the words of others. A parent who made love feel conditional. A partner who withheld affection until you performed just right. A teacher who embarrassed you in front of the class. A friend who betrayed you when you were vulnerable. For others, shame comes from within, born of silent expectations, internalized guilt, and a deep fear of not being enough. It is the voice that rises when you look in the mirror and wince. The feeling that follows you even after you have succeeded, whispering that you are still somehow failing. It is heavy and invisible, yet it influences how you speak, how you love, how you live.

Moving from shame to self-acceptance is one of the most courageous acts a person can undertake. It is not a single decision made in a moment of inspiration. It is a series of daily choices to believe in a better story. It means standing up to the voice that says you are unworthy and choosing to counteract that with the truth. It means seeing the mess, the mistakes, the moments you wish you could erase, and still saying, "I am loved." It means allowing yourself to be seen, not only in your strength, but in your weakness. Not only in your faith, but in your questions. Not only in your joy, but in your sorrow.

Self-acceptance is not about denial. It is not pretending that the past did not happen or that you have not made mistakes. It is about acknowledging all of it, owning your full story, and still choosing to believe that you are worthy of compassion, love, and healing. It is deciding that you will no longer let shame define who you are or who you are becoming. It is saying that you will no longer punish yourself for things you did not cause or could not control.

This process is rarely easy. There will be days when shame feels louder than truth. There will be moments when your old inner voice tries to return, dressed in false humility or even religious language. But the truth of God always stands in contrast to the lies of shame. God does not speak condemnation over you. He does not withhold His love until you have performed. He does not turn away when you fall. He moves closer. He draws near to the broken-hearted and binds up their wounds. He does not wait for you to be whole before He calls you His own.

As you begin to accept yourself, you may feel uncomfortable. You may feel undeserving. But grace does not operate on worthiness. Grace operates on truth. And the truth is, your worth was determined before you were born. It is not something you earn. It is something you already possess because of who created you and how deeply He loves you. Shame may speak loudly, but it cannot compete with the steady, healing voice of the Father who calls you by name and declares you enough.

Over time, self-acceptance becomes less about striving and more about resting. Resting in the knowledge that your story matters. Resting in the understanding that your healing is not dependent on your performance. It is in the reality that God is not disappointed in you. He delights in you. When you stop hiding, you stop hustling towards your worth, and you start walking in the truth that has always been yours.

You are not defined by your shame. You are not identified by your wounds. You are a beloved child of God, and your value has never changed. Your worth is not tarnished by trauma, not reduced by rejection, not canceled by mistakes. When you see yourself through the eyes of grace, you begin to rise. You begin to live. You begin to walk, not ashamed, but in freedom.

Freedom does not mean you forget what happened. It means what happened no longer gets to define what is true about you. And this is where the story begins to turn, because God does not only heal you for your comfort. He heals you for your wholeness, and He redeems what tried to destroy you.

How God Uses Brokenness

We do not often choose brokenness. It arrives without asking. It shatters the plans we carefully constructed. It interrupts the life we thought we were building. Sometimes it comes through sudden loss, other times through slow erosion, the kind that wears away at our souls one disappointment at a time.

It can leave us confused, hurting, and disoriented, unsure of who we are or where God is in the middle of it all. We ask the questions that echo in every wounded heart: Why did this happen? Why me? Why now? What could I have done differently?

And yet, in the middle of all the uncertainty, there is one thing that never changes: God does not waste brokenness. He does not sweep it aside. He does not look away from the mess. He does not turn His face from the shattered pieces. Instead, He steps into them. He gets close. He kneels in the dust of what remains and begins the work of redemption, not from a distance, but right in the middle of it. What looks like the end to us is often the beginning of something holy in the hands of God.

God does not restore in the way the world restores. He does not simply glue things back together and pretend they were never broken. He transforms. He reshapes. He rebuilds in a way that makes the broken places stronger and more beautiful than before.

He uses the cracks, the scars, and the jagged edges to tell a story of grace that could never have been told through a perfect life. He works through what we would rather forget and brings out what we could never create on our own wisdom, empathy, compassion, and a deeper dependence on Him.

The world teaches us to hide our brokenness, to cover it up with filters and smiles and polished answers. But God calls us to bring our whole selves to Him, not just the parts we think are acceptable. He calls us to lay it all down, every shattered dream, every silent scream, every unanswered question and trust that He is big enough to hold it. When we do, something powerful begins to happen. The broken places become meeting places. The ruins become altars. The pain becomes purposeful.

Your brokenness is not the end of your usefulness. It is not the thing that disqualifies you. It is the very place where God's presence becomes undeniable. It is the platform upon which your healing will stand. What the enemy intended for destruction, God will use for glory. The moments that nearly destroyed you will become testimonies of His power and faithfulness. The weakness you thought would ruin you will become the place where His strength is made perfect.

This does not mean that everything will be easy. It does not mean that we will always understand. There will still be grief. There will still be days when the ache rises unexpectedly. There will be times when you wonder if the healing is really working. But God does not ask you to understand everything. He asks you to trust Him in the process. He asks you to keep bringing the pieces to Him, even when they feel too sharp to hold. He asks you to believe that nothing you have been through is wasted in His hands.

God is not afraid of your brokenness. He is not intimidated by your wounds. He is not disappointed in your struggles. He is the God who chooses the broken to carry the message of wholeness. He chose Moses, who doubted his voice. He chose David, who carried deep regret. He chose Ruth, who had lost everything. He chose the woman at the well, who felt too ashamed to be seen. He chose Paul, who once persecuted those He would later lead. And He chooses you not despite your brokenness, but because of it.

There is a purpose in the breaking. There is something about the shattered places that opens us to the presence of God in ways that comfort never could.

When we are empty, He fills us.

When we are weak, He carries us.

When we are lost, He comes after us.

He never leaves us in the wreckage. He meets us there and begins to build something eternal from the fragments that will not just bring healing to you, but to others who will find hope through your story.

You do not have to hide what hurts you. You do not have to be ashamed of the broken places. They are the places where the light enters. They are the places where love becomes real. They are the places where God meets you with tenderness and says, "Let me show you what I can do with this." And what He builds from those broken pieces will not only surprise you, it will redeem you.

One of the ways brokenness tries to keep its grip is through hiding. When pain feels unsafe to reveal, we learn to manage impressions, to protect ourselves with performance, and to wear masks that keep people close but not too close. That is why surrendering the mask is not a separate part of healing. It is one of the most necessary parts.

The Beauty of Surrendering the Mask

Most of us learn very early how to hide. Not with a real mask, but with something that becomes just as familiar. We learn how to smile when we are hurting. How to stay quiet when everything inside us wants to speak. How to answer "I am fine" so easily that it starts to sound believable, even when our insides feel like they are unraveling. Over time, that mask becomes part of how we survive. It helps us move through a world that does not always feel safe, a world that often praises strength but feels uncomfortable with honesty.

We wear masks because they give us a sense of control. They help us show up looking strong, composed, and put together, even when we are anything but. We tell ourselves that if we can just keep the mask in place, no one will notice the fear, the pain, or the doubts beneath the surface. And for a while, it works. We stay busy. We keep going. We achieve. We serve. We show up for everyone else. But quietly, underneath it all, we are tired. And more than anything, we long for someone to truly see us and still stay.

There is a kind of beauty that only appears when we begin to take the mask off. It is not easy. It feels vulnerable and scary. We wonder what will happen if we let the truth show. What if we are misunderstood? What if we are rejected? What if who we really are feels like too much? But hiding has a cost. The longer we wear the mask, the further we drift from ourselves. We lose touch with our own hearts. We forget what it feels like to be honest and real. And healing cannot grow in places where hiding continues to live.

Letting go of the mask does not mean telling everyone everything. It does not mean having no boundaries or inviting the whole world into your most tender places. It means choosing honesty over performance. Truth over image. It means showing up as you are, without pretending that everything is okay when it is not. It means giving yourself permission to be seen, known, and loved, even in the places that still hurt.

God has never been interested in the mask. He already sees past it. He sees the version of you that you have worked so hard to hide. The one who cries when no one is watching. The one who questions her worth. The one who has carried more than she was ever meant to carry. And He does not turn away. He does not pull back. He draws closer. He meets you with compassion, not judgment. With tenderness, not shame.

When the mask comes off, space is created for something new. Space for rest. Space for connection. Space for healing. Relationships begin to feel different because they are no longer built on who you are pretending to be, but on who you truly are. You begin to hear your own voice again.

You begin to feel more deeply, not because you are weak, but because you are waking up. You start to believe that you do not have to earn love through performance.

There is beauty in being undone.

Beauty in tears that finally fall after being held back for so long.

Beauty in a trembling voice that tells the truth for the first time.

Beauty in the moment you stop apologizing for your emotions and start honoring them.

Beauty in choosing real over polished, depth over perfection, honesty over pretending.

Releasing the mask does not require full exposure to everyone. It begins with honesty with yourself and with God. It looks like no longer running from the parts of your story that still ache. It means allowing light into places you once kept hidden. And it means slowly believing that the real you, the one beneath the mask, is worthy of love, belonging, and grace.

The beauty of surrendering the mask is not only in what you let go of, but in what you gain. You gain clarity. You gain peace. You gain freedom to walk in truth without fear of being exposed. Because you are no longer hiding.

You are no longer pretending.

You are healing.

You are becoming.

Being Held in the Middle of the Mess

There is a part of the healing journey that feels the most vulnerable. It is not the beginning when you first admit the pain. It is not the end when restoration becomes visible. It is in the middle. The middle is where everything feels uncertain. It is full of unresolved questions, buried emotions, and uncomfortable truths.

It is the place where you are no longer who you were, but not yet who you are becoming. You have let go of the mask. You have named the hurt. But you still do not know what healing fully looks like. And that in-between space can feel lonely and terrifying.

This is where many people turn back. The temptation to pretend can be overwhelming. The discomfort of growth feels like too much. The silence becomes difficult to bear. In this place, you may wonder if God has stepped away. You may question if you have done something wrong. You may believe that healing is for other people and not for you.

These thoughts are honest. They are real. And they do not disqualify you from healing. They are a sign that you are doing the work. That you are beginning to feel what you once numbed. That you are letting yourself be human again.

Being held in the middle of the mess means learning to trust that you do not have to carry everything alone. It means allowing yourself to be supported, even if for now the only arms holding you belong to God. It means believing that just because it feels messy does not mean it is meaningless. The middle is not a void. The middle is where God is deeply present. Not because you have done something extraordinary, but because you have chosen to be real.

God does not wait until your story is tidy before He enters in. He does not love only the healed version of you. He does not call you worthy only when the pain is behind you. He is near now. He is near in the silence, in the questions, and in the ache that will not go away. He sees every tear that falls without witness. He hears the prayers that come out as nothing more than breath. He understands the days you feel numb, the nights you feel afraid, and the mornings you wish you could skip. He is not offended by your mess. He enters it with love.

There is something holy about being held when you feel you have nothing left to give. There is a freedom in allowing yourself to be supported when you are at your weakest. God does not withdraw when you fall apart. He draws closer. In the middle of the mess, His presence is not distant. It is tender. It is gentle. It surrounds you like a whisper you did not expect. He wraps you in grace when you feel undeserving. He covers you in mercy when shame wants to rise. He stays. Not only for healing. He stays for you.

Being held in the middle means you do not have to rush. You do not have to force your healing. You do not have to hurry toward answers. It means breathing when all you can do is breathe. It means resting when progress feels impossible. It means being kind to yourself when the voices in your head are cruel. It means remembering that your value does not increase with your productivity. You are worth loving as you are. Not as you will be. As you are.

There is something miraculous happening here, even if you cannot see it. Every time you choose truth over hiding, every time you let someone in, every time you whisper a prayer even in your doubt, something is shifting. The foundation beneath your feet is being rebuilt. The pieces are beginning to form something new. And one day, you will look back and see the beauty that was growing here. Not despite the mess. But in it.

You are not forgotten in this place. You are not invisible. You are not too much. You are not behind. You are being held. Not just by your own strength. But by the everlasting arms of a God who calls you beloved in every chapter. You do not have to figure everything out today. You do not have to be further along. You do not have to carry the weight of healing on your own. You only have to take the next breath, the next step, the next moment. And trust that God is holding you through it all.

You Are Not Alone in This

One of the cruelest lies pain will tell you is that you are the only one. It whispers that no one else has felt what you are feeling. That no one else would understand the weight you carry. That you are too broken, too far gone, too complicated to be reached. And when you are hurting, those lies feel convincing. They settle in like the truth and cause you to withdraw. You are isolated. You shut down. You stop reaching. You tell yourself it is safer that way. Safer to go through it alone than to risk being seen and rejected.

But isolation is not protection. It is a prison. And healing was never meant to happen in the dark.

You are not alone in this. You never were. Even when you cried yourself to sleep. Even when you whispered prayers you were not sure anyone was hearing. Even when you walked through moments of unbearable grief and unspeakable confusion. God was there. He has always been there.

In the quiet.

In the shadows.

In the pain.

In the spaces where you thought no one could possibly reach you, He was already there, waiting for you to realize that He never left.

There is something deeply healing about knowing you are not walking through this on your own. It does not mean that others will fully understand your journey. But it does mean you are not the only one navigating the wreckage. There are others who have felt what you are feeling. Others who are learning, just like you, how to live without the mask. How to let the broken places breathe. How to be honest about their pain and still move forward. You are not the only one learning how to grieve what was lost and embrace what is being restored.

God has placed people in this world who will walk beside you if you let them. People who do not need you to be perfect. People who have their own scars and their own stories. People who will hold your hand without trying to fix you. People who will sit in silence without demanding words. They exist. They are out there. Sometimes it takes courage to find them. Sometimes it takes vulnerability to let them in.

But you were not created for isolation. You were created for connection. For community. For love.

And more than anyone else, God will continue to be the steady presence in every part of this journey. He will be your strength when you are weak. He will be your peace when the storm returns. He will be your comfort when the ache rises unexpectedly. You do not have to earn His presence. You do not have to prove anything to deserve His love. He simply stays. In the pain. In the waiting. In the rebuilding.

You are not alone in your brokenness. You are not alone in your becoming. And you never will be.

Held in the Healing

Sometimes we spend so much time trying to hold everything together that we forget what it feels like to be held ourselves.

We become the strong one.

The dependable one.

The one who pushes through.

The one who smiles even when it hurts.

We become so accustomed to survival that when healing begins to ask for our softness, we do not know how to offer it. We try to schedule our pain. We try to manage our emotions. We try to heal without feeling. But true healing is not managed. It has surrendered. It is honest. It is slow, and it is sacred.

To be held in the healing is to let go of the illusion that you must do this alone. It is to recognize that God is not waiting for a more polished version of you before He wraps you in His love. He is not disappointed by your tears. He is not burdened by your weakness. He is not measuring your progress with a checklist. He is simply present. Here. Now. In the ache that lingers and the breath that shakes. He does not flinch at your wounds. He enters them. Not to rush you through, but to walk with you through every layer of what is surfacing.

Healing asks you to slow down. To listen to the parts of you you have ignored. To offer compassion to the younger version of yourself who learned how to survive by staying silent. It asks you to stop proving and start receiving. It asks you to believe, even when it feels impossible, that you are still worthy of love, even in places that have not yet healed.

You are not broken beyond repair. You are unfolding. You are learning how to let yourself be seen without the need to explain or defend. You are learning how to breathe again in spaces that once stole your air. You are remembering how it feels to be human. To be soft. To be seen. And to be loved in that seeing.

This reflection is not about fixing anything. It is about becoming aware of what is rising within you. It is about telling the truth without shame. It is about allowing grace to touch the places you have called unlovable and letting God speak a better word over them. You do not need to know the next step right now. You do not have to have it all figured out. You only need to be honest in this moment.

So, take a deep breath. Find stillness, if only for a few minutes. And ask your heart what it needs to say. Let your words rise without editing. Let your truth flow without fear.

If you take nothing else from this chapter, take this. You are not behind. You are not failing because it still hurts. You are not weak because some days you feel tender and unsure. Healing often looks like returning to the same places with new compassion. It looks like learning to speak to yourself with kindness. It looks like trusting that God is still working even when you cannot see results yet. You are not being punished by the process. You are being carried through it.

CHAPTER 4

FACING THE WOUNDS

When Silence Starts to Hurt

There is a kind of silence that does not bring rest. Not the quiet that settles over a soul in peace, but the heavy hush that lingers when you have gone too long without telling the truth. It is the silence that follows years of pushing pain down, of smiling when you wanted to cry, of pretending that certain moments did not pierce your heart. It is not just the absence of words, but the absence of permission to feel. I carried that kind of silence for years. I convinced myself it kept me safe. But deep down, it was choking the life out of me.

At first, it felt necessary. I had been taught, either directly or by the unspoken rules of the spaces I existed in, that strong people do not make a scene. That respectable women hold it together. That being good meant staying quiet. So, I became the peacemaker. The one who smoothed things over. The one who tucked her feelings away and smiled through discomfort. I trained myself to avoid conflict, to hide my disappointment, to never cause waves. Even when my heart was screaming that something was not right, my voice stayed locked inside my chest.

I thought I was doing the right thing. I told myself I was mature, that I was taking the high road, that I was being the bigger person. I excused the words that stung, the behaviors that crossed lines, the wounds that never really healed. I thought that if I just gave it enough time, the ache would go away. But the pain that is buried does not dissolve. It becomes part of you. It twists itself around your worth and whispers lies about who you are and what you deserve. That kind of silence is not noble. It is dangerous.

Eventually, the silence began to ache. Not just in my mind or in my emotions, but in my body. I could feel it in my chest, like a weight pressing down. I could feel it in the tension I carried on my shoulders, in the weariness that never quite left.

I could feel it in the way I kept showing up for everyone else but could not seem to show up for myself. I was disappearing slowly, and I was doing it with a smile on my face. I had become so used to neglecting my own voice that I almost forgot what it sounded like.

Somewhere along the way, I started to feel like a stranger in my own life. I was doing all the things I was supposed to do, being who I thought everyone needed me to be, but deep down, something essential was missing. I was present in my body but absent in my soul. I had learned how to perform, but I had lost connection with the truth of who I was. And the silence I had once used to survive was no longer just uncomfortable. It was unbearable.

I wish I could say there was one defining moment that changed everything. But the truth is, the shift came slowly.

It came in small moments of awakening. A conversation that left me hollow.

A memory that surfaced without warning. A whisper from God that landed deeper than usual. These moments felt insignificant on their own, but together they created a stirring, a realization that I could not keep living this way. I could not keep pretending that things did not hurt me. I could not keep offering peace to others while robbing myself of the same.

The most painful part was admitting that I had contributed to my own suffering. I had allowed others to speak to me in ways that were unkind, dismissive, or degrading. I had allowed their comfort to matter more than my dignity. I had told myself that my feelings were too much, that I was probably just being sensitive, that it was not worth the confrontation. But all of that left me fragmented. I had silenced myself for so long that even God's voice seemed faint. I began to realize that He had been speaking all along, but I had buried my pain so deeply that I could not hear Him clearly anymore.

There is something deeply holy about facing your pain. Not rushing past it. Not numbing it. Not justifying it. But truly sitting with it. Naming it. Giving yourself permission to weep over it. That is when healing begins. Not when everything is fixed, but when the truth is finally welcomed into the light. I began to write again. Not for anyone else, just for myself. I began to pray differently. Not polished prayers, but raw ones. I began to look at myself in the mirror with compassion instead of shame. I began to say what I needed instead of always asking what others needed from me.

And slowly, I began to feel again. The numbness lifted.

The sorrow found expression. The silence began to break.

It was not comfortable.

It was not easy.

But it was necessary.

Because the kind of silence that hides pain never leads to peace. It only deepens the wound. Real peace comes when the truth is given space to breathe.

I am learning that my voice matters. That my experiences are valid. That my feelings are not flaws. I am learning that God is not asking me to be silent to be holy. He is asking me to be honest. He is asking me to trust Him enough to bring every wound, every question, every ache into His presence. Not just the ones I have words for, but even the ones that still make me tremble. He meets me there. And in that place, He begins the beautiful work of healing.

The silence no longer owns me. I am no longer afraid of what will happen if I speak. I know now that healing begins with truth. And I am learning how to live in freedom of that truth, one brave word at a time.

Realizing What I Let Happen

There is a kind of heartbreak that does not come from what others do to you, but from what you allow to happen to yourself. I did not understand that at first. I had been so focused on surviving what was done to me that I had never stopped reflecting on the ways I had abandoned myself in the process. I thought the wounds were only caused by the word's others said, the actions they took, the moments they failed to protect or see me. But as I began to heal, I came face to face with a truth that brought both clarity and grief. I had allowed it. Not all of it. Not the original pain. But I stayed in places where the pain continued. I had silenced my own voice when I should have spoken. I had minimized what hurt me to protect people who never paused to consider how they were hurting me.

It was sobering to realize that some of my wounds were self-inflicted. Not because I was cruel to myself, but because I was too afraid to be kind to myself. I mistook silence for humility. I mistook avoidance for peace. I thought letting things go meant I was being gracious, but really, I was just disappearing. I was fading into the background of my own life while calling it strength. I thought if I let people say what they wanted, act how they wanted, and believe what they wanted about me, I was showing maturity. I was being the bigger person. But the truth was, I was shrinking.

There were conversations that left me in tears long after they ended. Words spoken to me in tones that should have never been used. Accusations that cut deep and assumptions that felt like judgment. And I took it. I took it with a forced smile and a nod of agreement, then went home and fell apart. I convinced myself that saying something would only make things worse. I told myself that maybe they were right. Maybe I was too sensitive. Maybe I was just being difficult. Maybe I deserved it.

Over time, those moments added up. One by one, they chipped away at my confidence, at my sense of identity, at my ability to trust my own voice. I let people treat me in ways that dishonored the image of God within me. And then I did something even more painful. I repeated their words in my own mind long after they had stopped speaking. I allowed their opinions to become my inner dialogue. I let their assumptions shape how I saw myself. I absorbed their disappointment as if it were truth.

And the hardest part of all was this. I let it happen because I believed that if I pushed back, I would lose them. I believed that love meant enduring. I believed that being worthy meant being agreeable. I believed that to be accepted, I had to make myself small enough to fit into the version of me they were comfortable with. So, I stayed quiet. I stayed compliant. I stayed invisible.

But at what cost?

There is a kind of grief that arises when you realize you have been complicit in your own silence. Not because you wanted to hurt yourself, but because you genuinely did not know another way. I had never been taught how to draw a boundary. I had never been told that it was not only okay, but necessary, to protect your peace. I had never seen what it looked like for a woman to say, "This is not acceptable," and still be seen as loving. I did not know I had permission to honor my own heart. So, I let it happen. Again, and again. Until something inside me said, no more.

That voice did not come in a shout. It came in a whisper. It came in quiet moments of reflection. It came in tears that I could not hold back anymore. It came in sleepless nights when I repeated conversations, wishing I had said something. It came in the exhausted breath I exhaled when I realized I had been keeping the peace at the cost of my own soul. And eventually, it became loud enough for me to hear.

It was the voice of the Holy Spirit. Not condemning me but inviting me to live differently. Inviting me to stop letting other people write the narrative of my life. Inviting me to take my voice back. Inviting me to step out of the shadows and into the light. I realized I had a choice. I could keep participating in my own pain by staying silent, or I could begin to participate in my healing by telling the truth.

And so, I started to look back, not to dwell, but to learn. I examined the patterns. I identified the places where I had consistently given people access to parts of me they had not earned. I looked at the conversations where I swallowed my voice to keep things calm. I acknowledged the ways I had tried to prove my worth instead of resting in it. I confessed the times I had ignored the still, small voice inside that whispered, this is not okay. I saw clearly, maybe for the first time, that I had not been protecting myself. I had been betraying myself.

But I also chose not to continue to live in shame. There was no healing in punishing myself for what I did not know back then. I extended compassion to the younger version of me who was simply trying to survive. I forgave myself for not being ready to speak when I was still learning how. I allowed myself to grieve the years lost to silence without letting that grief steal the possibility of restoration. I chose to honor the woman I was becoming, one brave decision at a time.

Realizing what I let happen did not break me. It opened the door to redemption. It was the beginning of returning to myself. And it gave me the courage to begin again, this time with truth in my mouth and grace in my heart.

When Holy Boldness Rose Up

I did not see it coming. That moment of holy boldness did not announce itself with a trumpet or send a warning sign to prepare me. It came quietly. It came without fanfare. It came in the middle of an ordinary day and a familiar situation; the kind I had experienced countless times before. I was sitting in a room with someone I deeply loved and respected, watching another person speak to her in a way that felt sharp, unfair, and unkind. My stomach tightened, my hands grew still, and my mind began to swirl with all the things I wanted to say but never had the courage to voice. I had been here before. So many times.

Normally, I would stay silent. I would go inward. I would convince myself that it was not my place, that I might make things worse, that perhaps I was overreacting or misinterpreting what was happening. I would wait until later to fall apart, letting the sadness and anger wash over me in the privacy of my own space. But this time was different. This time something rose up inside of me, and I could not ignore it. It was not just emotion. It was not just a reaction. It felt sacred. It felt like fire.

I spoke. It was not loud. It was not aggressive. But it was sure and firm. My words came out steady, full, and clear. They did not tremble like they usually did. They did not trail themselves off into apologies or soften themselves to make others more comfortable. I did not rehearse what I was going to say. I did not try to make it perfect. I simply said what needed to be said. I stood up for the woman in the room who was being spoken to as if her dignity was disposable. And in doing so, I realized I was standing up for the part of myself that had remained silent for far too long.

I was not combative. I was not cruel. I was not looking to pick a fight. I was simply tired. Tired of watching moments pass that should have been confronted. Tired of walking away, filled with regret. Tired of carrying the weight of conversations I never entered because I was afraid of what people would think. I had no desire to be reckless with my words, but I also could no longer afford to be careless with my silence. It cost me too much.

In that moment, something holy took over. Something brave. Something deep. It was not pride. It was not ego. It was a kind of righteousness that I had never experienced before. Not self-righteousness. But the kind that rises when truth and love intertwine and give birth to courage. It was sacred ground. And I knew it.

For the first time in a long time, I did not go home and replay the conversation in my head. I did not lie awake wondering what I should have said. I did not spiral into self doubt or regret. I spoke with clarity. I had spoken with love. I had spoken with truth. And I was not ashamed. That alone was a miracle.

There was something so unfamiliar about not questioning myself afterward. I had become so used to second guessing, so conditioned to apologizing for my presence, so programmed to make myself smaller that confidence felt foreign. But it also felt familiar in a strange way. As if I was meeting a version of myself that had always been there, waiting quietly in the background, waiting for permission to speak. She was not new. She was home.

That boldness did not come from me alone. I know that without a doubt. It came from the Spirit of God within me. It came from the long hours I had spent on my knees. It came from the quiet prayers whispered through tears. It came from the deep work of healing that had begun long before that moment. It was the fruit of surrender, the evidence of something shifting within. It was the beginning of a new way of living.

Everything in me had been trained to believe that using my voice would lead to rejection. That speaking the truth would drive people away. That drawing a line would make me difficult or unloving. But what I discovered was something entirely different. When your voice is rooted in truth and covered in grace, it becomes a vessel for healing. Not just for you, but for others as well. It invites honesty. It opens doors. It exposes what needs to change and offers a pathway toward restoration.

I realized that speaking up was not the enemy of peace. Silence was. Not the silence of reflection or wisdom, but the silence that comes from fear, from shame, from years of believing that your voice does not matter. That kind of silence poisons relationships. It corrodes self-worth. It allows harmful patterns to thrive in the shadows. But when boldness rises, when truth is spoken in love, chains begin to fall.

Patterns begin to break. People begin to heal.

After that moment, I noticed how often I had kept myself quiet to keep others comfortable. How often I had prioritized their emotions over my own truth. How often I had smiled through pain to avoid being misunderstood. And I grieved that. I grieved the parts of myself I had silenced. I grieved the girl who had learned that being agreeable was safer than being honest. But I also celebrated. Because she was beginning to speak again.

That one moment of boldness changed everything. It reminded me of who I am. It reminded me of who God created me to be. Not someone who steam rolls over others or speaks just to be heard, but someone who tells the truth with tenderness. Someone who uses her voice to build bridges, not burn them. Someone who refuses to let fear decide when and how she will show up in the world.

And this was just the beginning.

I carried that boldness into other spaces. I began to speak up more often, not with arrogance, but with assurance. I began to say no when something crossed the boundary of what was healthy or kind. I began to say yes to conversations that honored truth and invited growth. I began to trust that my voice, when used with wisdom and love, was a gift, not a problem.

Holy boldness is not about always being right. It is about being willing. Willing to step into uncomfortable spaces when love calls you there. Willing to risk misunderstanding for the sake of truth. Willing to stop performing and start living. It is not the absence of fear. It is choosing to move forward despite it.

And once you experience it, once you feel that fire rise and hear your own voice ringing with conviction, you cannot go back. You might still tremble. You might still question. But you will never believe the lie that your silence is safer than your truth. You will never again settle for being unseen and unheard. You will know what it means to be free.

The Day Everything Shifted

When I spoke up that first time, I thought the world might fall apart. I genuinely believed that everything would come crashing down. I was bracing for rejection. I was preparing for a backlash. I thought I would be punished for stepping outside of the role I had always played. That is what shame teaches you. That is what fear convinces you to expect. For so long, I had told myself that silence was what held everything together, that if I kept the peace, then maybe nothing would break. But the truth was, the silence had been breaking me all along.

What happened instead was quieter than I expected. There was no explosion. There was no dramatic unraveling. There was simply a shift. Something invisible but undeniable. Something that began in my soul and moved outward into every corner of my life. When I spoke, when I chose truth over comfort, something inside me clicked into place. A piece of myself that had been scattered came back. It was as if the foundation beneath my feet began to take shape again, not built on pleasing others or avoiding conflict, but built on integrity, honesty, and inner peace.

And as I began to live from that place, everything around me started to respond. Not always in ways I expected or hoped for, but in ways that revealed who was meant to walk with me into this next chapter and who was not. Some relationships grew quiet. Some faded completely. Not because I pushed people away, not because I became bitter or angry, but because I stopped performing. I stopped bending myself to fit into boxes I had long outgrown. I stopped apologizing for my boundaries and started honoring my growth. I was not interested in pretending anymore, and that made some people uncomfortable.

There were moments when that hurt deeply. Letting go of familiar connections, even unhealthy ones, is never easy. I missed the comfort of old rhythms, even the ones that caused pain. I missed being understood, even if that understanding came at the expense of my wholeness. I missed the approval I had once earned by staying silent. But I also knew that staying in those places would cost me something far more valuable. My peace. My voice. My healing.

So, I kept going.

I started setting boundaries, real ones. Not angry walls built from resentment, but intentional lines drawn from a place of wisdom and love. I began to discern the difference between grace and enabling, between compassion and self-sacrifice. I started to recognize when I was being drained instead of encouraged, when I was being manipulated instead of respected. I no longer felt the need to explain or defend every decision I made. I simply trusted that God was teaching me how to protect the sacred work He was doing in me. And that meant not everyone could have the same access they once did.

Some people were surprised. Some were offended. Some distanced themselves quietly. And while that stung, I had to remind myself that people who only loved the version of me that stayed quiet were never truly loving me. They loved the parts of me that made their lives easier. They loved the convenience of my silence. And I was done living for that kind of love. I wanted something deeper. I wanted relationships rooted in truth, in mutual respect, in grace that flows both ways.

Not all the shifts were painful. Some were beautiful. As I began to step into my voice, I began to discover just how many people were longing for someone to do the same. I started to find community with people who valued honesty, who celebrated growth, who were not threatened by boundaries but honored them. I found friends who held space for hard conversations, who did not flinch when I was real, who reminded me that healing is not something we do alone. These relationships did not require me to shrink. They invited me to be seen.

I also noticed something else. The more I used my voice for myself, the more I began to use it for others. Not in a savior complex kind of way, but in a spirit-led way. I felt a stirring to speak up for those who had not yet found their words. For the ones who were still sitting in rooms where they felt invisible. For the ones who did not yet know that their boundaries were sacred. For the ones who had learned, like I once did, that their silence was the price they had to pay to be loved.

It was not about being loud or confrontational. It was about being rooted. It was about being aligned with the truth. I began to see that my boldness was not prideful. It was not rebellious. It was redemptive. It was the fruit of healing. It was a marker of freedom. I was no longer trying to win approval. I was walking in purpose. And that purpose included using my voice in ways that reflected the love of God and the truth of who I was in Him.

That shift was everything.

It did not fix all my problems. It did not make relationships effortless. It did not erase the discomfort of being misunderstood. But it brought peace. The kind of peace that only comes from living in alignment with your values. The kind of peace that comes when your words match your heart. The kind of peace that stays, even when others leave.

I was no longer performing. I was no longer trying to keep the world calm by keeping myself small. I had stepped out of the shadows and into the light of who God was calling me to be. And while that light sometimes revealed things I would rather not see, it also illuminated beauty I had long forgotten existed.

My strength.

My wisdom.

My voice.

My worth.

Everything shifted. Not in one dramatic moment, but in a hundred small ones. Every time I spoke when it would have been easier to stay silent. Every time I chose peace with God over peace with people. Every time I honored the healing He was doing in me instead of hiding it. Every time I refused to go back to the version of me that I had learned to survive by disappearing.

I could finally breathe.

I could finally rest.

I could finally live.

Participation in My Healing

Healing, for a long time, felt like something that would happen to me. I waited for it as if it were a package arriving on my doorstep, handed to me by God in a single sacred moment that would erase all the pain and confusion.

I prayed for that kind of healing. I begged for it. I pleaded in whispered prayers through sleepless nights, asking God to take the ache away, to make the sorrow stop, to free me from the heaviness that followed me like a shadow.

And while there were moments when His presence brought immediate comfort, what I learned is that healing is rarely instant. It is not something that dropped into our laps while we remain passive recipients.

Healing is an invitation. It is something God invites us into, something He walks with us through, but not something He forces. He will never drag us into healing. He waits for our yes. And then He takes that yes, even if it is whispered with trembling lips, and begins the holy work of restoration.

I had to stop waiting for the healing to come without my participation. I had to stop expecting God to do all the work while I stayed hidden behind fear and self-protection. There was a turning point in my journey where I realized that I had a part to play. I was not a Healer, but I was not powerless either. I had to show up. I had to be willing to look inward. I had to bring the pain into the light. That was my part.

Healing requires courage. Not the kind of courage that always demands perfection or strength, but the quiet kind.

The kind that says I am willing to face what I have been avoiding.

The kind that says I will no longer numb or deny what is still hurting. The kind that says I choose growth even when it feels uncomfortable. That kind of courage, I learned, is the birthplace of transformation.

When I look at Scripture, I see this pattern again and again. Jesus healed many, but often He asked them to do something first. He told the man with the withered hand to stretch it out. He told the lame man to get up and carry his mat. He told the blind man to go wash in the pool. There was always a response required. Not because the response itself held power, but because faith expresses itself in movement. And in the movement, something begins to stir.

God began to show me that I could not be passive in my own healing. I had to be a willing participant. I had to bring the wounds to Him. I had to say what I had kept buried. I had to take steps, even small ones, toward wholeness. Some of those steps were difficult. Some of them felt like walking through fire. But each one was necessary.

Some days, participation looked like writing down what I was too afraid to say out loud. Pouring the raw, unfiltered truth onto paper in a journal that only God and I would ever read. Other days, it looked like saying no when I would normally have said yes. Not out of defiance, but out of self-respect. Sometimes it meant speaking honestly in conversations where I had once gone silent. Sometimes it meant resting, doing nothing but letting God hold me in the quiet. Each step, no matter how small, became a sacred offering.

I also had to confront the beliefs that had kept me stuck. Beliefs like I had to earn healing, that I had to be good enough, that I had to get everything right before I could be restored. I had to let go of the idea that healing was a reward and embrace the truth that healing is a gift. One that God offers not because we deserve it, but because He is good. One that requires our surrender more than our strength.

Participation in my healing also meant allowing others to walk with me. This was one of the hardest parts. I had spent so much of my life being the strong one, the steady one, the one who held space for others but never asked for anything in return. Inviting others into my process felt vulnerable. But I realized that isolation breeds shame, and shame thrives in secrecy.

Healing, on the other hand, blossoms in community. In safe, honest spaces where you are seen and still loved. Where you are heard and not dismissed. Where you can be both hurting and hopeful, and no one tries to rush you through your process.

Letting others in did not mean sharing everything with everyone. It meant being prayerful and discerning about who could hold my heart with care. It meant finding people who would not try to fix me, but who would sit with me. Who would remind me of God's truth when I forgot. Who would encourage me when I wanted to give up. That, too, was participation. Choosing connection instead of isolation. Choosing honesty instead of hiding.

There were also practical steps that became part of my healing. Creating space in my schedule to rest. Making room for the things that brought joy. Limiting conversations that left me drained. Releasing guilt that was never mine to carry. Practicing gratitude when the weight of sorrow felt suffocating. Speaking the truth out loud when fear tried to settle in again. None of it was grand or dramatic. It was slow. It was intentional. It was daily. And that is what made it powerful.

Healing did not happen in one moment. It happened in many moments. The quiet ones. The messy ones. The courageous ones. The ones where I fell and got back up again. It happened each time I chose to show up to my own story with compassion instead of criticism. Each time I turned to God instead of running from Him. Each time I stopped pretending and allowed myself to be fully seen.

God never asked me to heal myself. He never demanded that I fix what was broken. He simply invited me to come. To bring my truth. To bring my tears. To bring my past and my pain and my questions. And to trust that He would do what only He can do.

My role was to show up, participate and be willing. And His role was to restore, rebuild. And to redeem. That was the partnership. That was the invitation.

And I said yes.

To the Woman Still Afraid to Face It

If you are reading this and feel a tightening in your chest, a heaviness that you cannot explain, or a quiet ache that surfaces when no one else is around, I want you to know this part is for you. You may be holding your breath as you turn each page, unsure of what emotions might rise. You may be whispering to yourself, I am not ready. Or maybe you are thinking, I do not even know where to begin. You are not alone. I see you. More importantly, God sees you.

I know what it feels like to live with a wound you have never named. To carry pain that has never been acknowledged. To walk through life with a smile on your face and a storm in your soul. I know what it is like to be so afraid of the pain that you convince yourself it is easier not to look at it. You tell yourself you are over it. You tell yourself you have moved on. You tell yourself it does not affect you anymore. But late at night, when the world is quiet, the truth comes knocking again.

Facing the pain feels terrifying because it requires you to stop running. It asks you to stop numbing. It invites you to stop hiding behind busy schedules and endless responsibilities. It calls you to slow down long enough to hear the cry of your own heart. And that is no small thing. It takes courage to feel. It takes bravery to remember. It takes trust to let God into the places you have tried to keep sealed shut.

But here is what I want to tell you. You are not weak for hurting. You are not broken beyond repair. You are not dramatic or overly sensitive or too much. You are human. You are someone who has walked through things that left a mark. You are someone who has learned to survive in ways that made sense at the time. And now, you are invited to do more than survive. You are invited to heal.

Healing will not always look like you thought it would. It may not come in a flood of emotion or in one defining moment. It may come slowly, like dawn breaking over a dark horizon. It may come in layers, in waves, in pieces. And that is okay. There is no right timeline. There is no formula. There is only honesty. One honest moment at a time. One honest prayer at a time. One honest step forward at a time.

You do not need to have it all figured out. You do not need to know how the story ends before you start walking. You just need to be willing. Willing to pause and say, God, I want to be whole. Willing to lay down the belief that your pain is too messy for Him. Willing to believe that even this, even what you have never said out loud, is not too much for His love.

Maybe you have spent years minimizing your pain because someone told you it was not that bad. Maybe you were taught to be strong, to be silent, to press on without complaint. Maybe you were told that talking about the past is pointless or that forgiveness means forgetting.

Maybe your survival depended on pretending it did not hurt. And now, the very idea of looking back feels like betrayal. But I want you to know that facing the pain is not betrayal. It is brave and it is necessary.

You are not defined by what happened to you. But you are allowed to acknowledge it. You are allowed to say it mattered. You are allowed to admit it left a scar. That does not mean you are stuck in the past. It means you are honoring your story. It means you are making room for healing to take root in truth, not denial. And that truth will set you free.

You are allowed to feel. To grieve. To cry over what you never had, what you lost, and what you needed but did not receive. You are allowed to feel anger and confusion. You are allowed to wrestle with it all. And in that place, you are allowed to be held by a God who is not overwhelmed by any part of your story.

He is not afraid of your pain. He does not flinch at your wounds. He is not disappointed by your emotions. He is not surprised by your story. He is the One who saw every moment, every tear, every whispered prayer you never thought reached heaven. He was there when you were hurting, and He is here now, calling you back to life.

Healing is not about pretending the past did not happen. It is about allowing God to breathe new life into it. It is about letting Him redeem what was broken. It is about trading shame for grace, sorrow for joy, bitterness for freedom. It is about becoming whole from the inside out, not because of what you do, but because of what He has done and is still doing.

You may not feel strong right now. That is okay. You do not have to be strong to start. You just have to be honest. You just have to say yes to healing, even if your voice trembles when you say it. God does not need your perfection. He desires your presence. He desires your willingness to open the door, even just a little, so He can begin the work only He can do.

And when you are ready, when your heart begins to whisper that it is time, I want you to remember this. You are not walking alone. There are others who have faced their wounds and found freedom on the other side. There are women who have stood where you are, afraid and unsure, and who are now walking in wholeness, not because they had all the answers, but because they said yes to the journey.

You are not a burden. You are not too complicated. You are not too far gone. You are loved. You are seen. You are pursued by a God who specializes in restoration. You are worthy of healing. You are worthy of peace. You are worthy of love that does not ask you to stay small or silent.

So, breathe. Let yourself exhale. Let yourself rest on the truth that you do not have to carry this alone. The One who holds all things together is holding you. And He is not letting go.

What the Wound Is Teaching

As you close this chapter, I want to invite you to pause and truly take in the journey you just walked through. Facing your wounds is not easy. It is tender, it is sacred, and it requires a depth of courage that few will ever fully understand. But if you made it this far, even if you read through tears or hesitation, even if you had to stop and breathe along the way, that is evidence of strength. That is evidence of growth. Healing does not demand perfection. It simply invites you to show up. And you did.

Let this be a moment where you stop judging your progress and begin honoring your courage. Let this be a space where you stop running from your story and begin standing in it with grace. God is not finished with you. He is just getting started.

The truth you are beginning to embrace will become the foundation of your freedom. And every brave choice to feel, to speak, and to release is building something beautiful in you.

You are not the same woman who began this chapter.

You are becoming. And your healing matters.

CHAPTER 5

STEPPING INTO CONFIDENCE

There is a kind of confidence that does not announce itself when it walks into the room. It does not need to shout or prove or posture. It does not perform. Instead, it rests. It anchors. It gently wraps itself around your shoulders like a cover that was always meant for you, even if you spent years believing it belonged to someone else. This kind of confidence does not come from applause or attention. It is not born out of perfection. It comes from knowing who you are. And more than that, it comes from knowing who your Creator is.

I did not always have that kind of confidence. For most of my life, I mistook it for something else. I thought confidence looked impressive. Like having all the right words, the endless ability to handle whatever was thrown my way. I thought it meant staying composed, being liked, staying small enough not to ruffle feathers but strong enough to be admired. So, I put on a performance. I got good at it. I smiled when I wanted to cry. I served when I felt empty. I stayed quiet when I had something to say, just to keep the peace. I was the one others could count on, but deep down, I didn't even know how to count on myself.

I spent years looking for affirmation from the outside, hoping that if I did enough, loved enough, or gave enough, I would eventually feel worthy. But no matter how much I gave, I always felt like I was one misstep away from unraveling. One moment of weakness away from being exposed. That is the thing about trying to build confidence on performance. It is fragile. It cracks under the weight of life. It shatters when you finally realize that who you are pretending to be is not who you truly are.

God began to show me that the version of confidence I had been chasing was not real. It was an illusion clothed in achievement and approval. It had no roots. No depth. It was dependent on circumstances, on other people, on a fragile sense of self that I had pieced together from the scraps of what I thought others needed from me. That was not confidence. That was survival. And I was tired of just surviving.

The real shift came slowly. It did not crash into my life. It unfolded gently, almost unnoticeably at first. It started in quiet places. In the broken places. In the moments when I could no longer carry the weight of who I was trying to be. I had to let something fall apart in order to let something truer rise from the wreckage.

I began to peel back the layers. I sat with the parts of myself I had ignored. I listened to the ache beneath the surface. I asked hard questions. I let myself feel the shame I had buried, the fear I had denied, the exhaustion I had ignored. I stopped running. I stopped pretending. I got still.

And in that stillness, I found something startling. I found strength.

It was not a loud strength. It was not the kind that needed to be seen. It was quiet. Unassuming. But it had weight to it. It had survived more than I gave it credit for. It had endured heartbreak, betrayal, silence, and grief. It had risen from ashes I never thought I would get out of. It had held me together when everything else fell apart. And in that strength, I began to recognize the beginnings of a new kind of confidence.

It did not rush in. It did not demand anything from me. It simply invited me to rest in who I truly was. It asked me to believe that I was already enough, even if I was still healing. It whispered that my worth had never been tied to my performance but had always been secured in the heart of God.

I started to feel it in small ways. In how I held my head a little higher. In how I answered questions without shrinking. In how I walked into the rooms without apologizing for taking up space. In how I stopped feeling like I had to overexplain or overcompensate just to be seen as worthy. I was not trying to prove anything anymore. I was simply showing up as myself, and that was enough.

This confidence came from knowing who I was, but more importantly, it came from knowing who I belonged to. It came from my identity being rooted in something eternal, something unchanging. The world had given me so many labels, so many definitions of who I was supposed to be. But God was gently peeling those off, reminding me of who He had always seen me as. Strong. Capable. Redeemed.

There was no dramatic moment when I declared that I had found my confidence. It did not feel like crossing a finish line. It felt more like returning home. Coming back to a part of myself that had always been there, just waiting to be acknowledged.

Waiting to be embraced.

Waiting to be trusted.

The most beautiful part of this journey was that the confidence I found was not prideful. It was the fruit of healing. The result of surrender. The outcome of facing the pain I used to run from and allowing God to turn it into something holy. I no longer needed to chase validation because I had finally received something far greater. I had received wholeness.

I learned that confidence is not the absence of fear or doubt. It is the courage to keep showing up anyway. It is the decision to walk in truth, even when you feel uncertain. It is the willingness to stand firm in your identity, even when others do not understand it. It is the steady belief that you are becoming who you were always created to be, and that becoming does not require permission from anyone else.

That confidence had been waiting for me all along. It was not hiding. I had simply been too busy trying to be everything for everyone else to recognize it. But now I see it clearly. I feel it rise in me when I speak with conviction. I sense it when I look in the mirror and see someone I finally recognize.

This is the kind of confidence that heals.

That frees.

That restores.

The kind that cannot be shaken by other people's opinions or destroyed by difficult seasons. It is the kind that remains because it is built on a foundation that never shifts. It is built on grace. It is built on truth. It is built on the love of a God who knew me, chose me, and called me worthy before I ever did a single thing to earn it.

And now that I have tasted it, I will never settle for anything less again.

Coming Out Of Hiding

When you have spent so much of your life hiding, stepping into the light does not always feel like freedom, it feels like exposure. The light is almost too much at first, like it burns your eyes. Being noticed makes you feel vulnerable, tender. Every look in your direction, every question asked, feels like a test you did not study for. Because for so long, you have taught yourself to shrink. To be quiet. To blend in. You learned that safety lived in invisibility.

I had grown used to the shadows. They were familiar. Predictable. Safe. I knew how to navigate them. I knew how to tuck away the parts of me that might be too much. I knew how to smile when I was breaking inside. I knew how to make everyone comfortable, even if it meant suffocating the truth of who I was.

The shadows gave me room to breathe in a world that often felt too loud and too demanding. But the truth is, I was not breathing. I was holding my breath. Waiting for permission to exhale. Waiting for someone to say it was okay to be me.

But that permission never came. Not from others. Not even from myself. I was the one who had locked myself in that place of hiding. And I was the only one who could choose to come out of it.

What people often misunderstand is that hiding is not always obvious. Sometimes it looks like being the helpful one.

The reliable one.

The selfless one.

It looks like blending in so well that you forget how to stand out. It looks like suppressing your opinions to avoid conflict. Like saying yes when your whole body is begging you to say no. Like dressing down your personality so that no one feels threatened by your presence. Like staying silent when you have something powerful to say because you are afraid of being misunderstood.

There were dreams I locked away because they felt too risky to speak out loud. Pieces of my identity I kept hidden because they had been met with criticism or confusion. Joy that I refused to hold onto because I believed it would not last. Opinions I swallowed to keep the peace. Pain, I denied because I thought it made me weak.

But the more I healed, the more I felt something stirring inside me. A quiet longing. A discomfort. I was no longer content with hiding. Not from the world, and not from myself. I began to sense that the parts of me I had buried were not dead.

They were waiting.

Waiting to be welcomed.

Waiting to be seen.

Waiting to come alive.

At first, I tested the water. I shared small parts of myself. I spoke up in conversations where I would have normally stayed quiet. I let myself dream without editing. I said what I needed instead of waiting for someone to guess. I asked for help without an apology. I started taking up space, not in a loud or demanding way, but in a grounded and honest one. I showed up as myself.

And people noticed. Some were surprised. Some did not know what to do with this version of me. Some quietly drifted away. But others leaned in. They were drawn not to perfection, but to authenticity. They resonated with the woman who had learned to show up with her truth intact. Not everyone celebrated my emergence, but I was not stepping into the light for applause. I was stepping into it for freedom.

There was something special about owning my voice. It did not feel like arrogance. It felt like alignment. It felt like I was finally walking in step with the woman God had always seen me as. The one who had strength even in her softness. The one who had wisdom shaped by fire. The one who had something to say, and the courage to say it. I was not performing anymore. I was simply being.

And being was enough.

I realized that my presence was not a problem. My truth was not a burden. My dreams were not too big. My feelings were not too much. I was not too much. I was just enough. I began to unlearn the idea that I needed to make others comfortable at the expense of my own soul.

I stopped shrinking so that others could shine.

I stopped apologizing for being seen.

I stopped hiding the very parts of me that made me whole.

It was not always easy. There were moments when I wanted to retreat. Moments when someone's reaction made me question if I had done the right thing by stepping forward. But every time I returned to the shadows, even briefly, I felt the weight of that old silence pressing in. I knew I could not stay there anymore. I had outgrown the place where I once found safety.

This was no longer about impressing others. It was about honoring the truth God had placed inside me. The truth is that I had value, even when I was quiet. That I had worth, even when I was unseen. But also, I had every right to come forward. To be known. To take up the space that had always been mine.

The more I showed up, the stronger I became. Not because I had it all together, but because I had finally stopped hiding the parts of me that were still healing. I began to believe that being vulnerable was not a weakness. It was a sign of courage. It was an act of trust. It was an invitation for others to do the same. There is something powerful about walking in your truth. It gives other people permission to walk in theirs.

I began to surround myself with people who celebrated the real me. Not just the version who helped them or served them or made their lives easier. But the version of me who laughed loudly. Who cried freely. Who dreamed boldly. Who said no without guilt. Who said yes without fear. People who could hold space for my fullness, not just my function.

Coming out of hiding did not mean I no longer needed boundaries. It meant I finally understood my worth enough to set them. It meant I trusted myself to know when I was safe and when I was not. When to speak and when to walk away. When to stand still and when to move forward.

And every time I chose to step into the light, I remembered that I was not alone. God was there, holding space for my unfolding. Whispering reminders of who I was. Reminding me that I did not have to earn my belonging. I already belonged. I belonged to Him. I belonged to myself. I belonged to this moment, fully awake, fully alive, fully seen.

Coming out of hiding was not just about being visible. It was about being whole. And now that I have tasted that kind of freedom, I will never go back to silence again.

Protecting My Peace

Peace is not something you stumble upon. It is not accidental, and it is not passive. It is a gift, but it is also a responsibility. There was a time in my life when I believed peace was only possible when everything around me was calm. I thought I had to wait for circumstances to be settled or for people to approve before I could feel at ease. But I have come to learn that peace is something you must fight for. It is something you must choose. And sometimes, it is something you must protect with everything you have.

Before healing began to shape my life, my inner world was noisy. I was constantly absorbing the emotions of others. If someone around me was angry, I felt responsible.

If someone was disappointed, I bent over backwards to make it right. If someone misunderstood me, I stayed up at night replaying every word I had said, wondering how I could fix it. I carried the weight of everyone else's feelings as if they were my own, and in the process, I lost touch with my own soul.

I was not at peace. I was constantly on edge, constantly second-guessing, constantly giving more of myself than I had to offer. I called it love. I called it loyalty. I called it being a good person. But it was not love if it came at the cost of my identity. It was not loyalty if it silenced my voice. It was not good if it left me empty. It was co-dependency. It was self abandonment. It was a slow erosion of my peace.

When healing entered my life, it did not only bring relief. It brought clarity. I began to recognize the patterns that had shaped me for so long. I saw how much I had sacrificed to keep other people comfortable. I noticed how quickly I would dismiss my own needs just to avoid conflict. I realized that my peace had always been negotiable, and that was the reason I never truly felt safe in my own skin.

But something began to shift. As I healed, I began to experience a stillness I had never known. A quietness in my spirit that did not depend on the behavior of others. A steadiness that came not from external validation, but from internal alignment. It felt like breathing for the first time after years of suffocation. And once I experienced that kind of peace, I knew I could never go back to the chaos I had once accepted as normal.

I decided. I would protect my peace, even if it cost me approval. I would protect my peace, even if it meant disappointing others. I would protect my peace, even if it meant walking away from relationships that were no longer healthy. I had spent too many years forfeiting my peace in the name of being polite, agreeable, or dependable. That season was over. I owed it to myself and to the work God was doing in me to hold my peace with reverence.

That meant I had to start setting boundaries. Real ones. Not just polite suggestions, but firm and clear limits that honored my healing. I had to learn that it was not cruel to say no. It was not selfish to need space. It was not wrong to expect respect. I had to stop apologizing for taking care of my soul. I had to stop offering explanations every time I needed rest or solitude. I had to give myself permission to protect what God was restoring in me.

Some people did not understand. Some resisted the new boundaries. They were used to the version of me who always said yes, who always made room, who always picked up the pieces. And in some ways, I missed her too.

She was familiar.

She was easy to love.

But she was also exhausted.

She was broken.

She was desperate for rest. And I could no longer betray her just to keep others happy.

I began to evaluate my relationships through a new lens. Not everyone could come with me into the new season of peace. Not because I stopped loving them, but because I started loving myself enough to acknowledge what was no longer life-giving. I stopped chasing after those who had never truly seen me. I stopped explaining myself to people who were committed to misunderstanding me. I stopped trying to earn love by sacrificing my well-being.

Instead, I leaned into relationships that felt safe and mutual. I poured into people who celebrated my growth, not just tolerated it. I welcomed those who saw me clearly and loved me deeply, not because of what I could give, but simply because of who I was. I let go of the guilt that had convinced me I had to keep everyone close. I realized that healthy love makes room for boundaries. It does not punish you for protecting your peace.

I began listening more closely to the voice of the Holy Spirit. That quiet whisper in my spirit that often nudged me before my mind caught up. I started trusting that voice. I paid attention to the places and people that disrupted my peace, and I stopped ignoring those red flags. I realized that peace is often the presence of God, and anything that constantly pulls me out of that presence is something I need to examine.

This was not about building walls. It was about building wisdom. It was about knowing when to lean in and when to walk away. When to speak and when to be silent. When to stay and when to move. It was about learning that my peace is not a luxury. It is a necessity. It is not optional. It is essential to my healing, to my growth, to my calling.

Peace became my compass. If something repeatedly stirred confusion, anxiety, or dread in my spirit, I paid attention. If someone consistently drained me or made me feel small, I created space. Not out of spite, but out of obedience to what God was showing me. Protecting my peace meant protecting the environment where healing could continue. Where clarity could grow. Where I could hear from God without all the noise.

There were still days when I questioned myself. When old patterns tried to rise again. When guilt knocked on the door. But I reminded myself that peace was a promise. Jesus said He would leave His peace with us. Not the fragile peace the world offers, but a deep and enduring peace that anchors our souls. And if He promised it, I was allowed to receive it. I was allowed to live in it. I was allowed to protect it.

Now, peace is not just something I hope for. It is something I walk in. It is a daily choice. A set boundary. A place where I meet with God and remember who I am.

I no longer let chaos dictate the condition of my soul.

I no longer let others decide my worth.

I no longer hand over my peace just to be accepted. I carry it like a flame that must be tended, sheltered, and honored.

Because this peace is not just for me. It is a testimony. A witness to what God can do when we stop surviving and start healing. When we stop hiding and start living. When we stop giving away our peace and start protecting it like the treasure it truly is.

The Fear of Going Back

Healing is beautiful, but it is also vulnerable. There is something fragile about it at first, like new skin after a wound has scabbed over. You know you are stronger than you were, but sometimes you are not sure if that strength will hold. You want to believe you have moved forward, that you have grown, that you are becoming new. And yet, there are moments when the fear whispers softly in the background, asking what you will do if you find yourself slipping back into old patterns.

That fear visited me more often than I liked to admit. Even as I found myself walking with more clarity and confidence, there were still echoes of the past that tried to pull me back. Memories of who I used to be. The version of me that stayed silent to keep the peace.

The one who sacrificed her own needs to feel loved.

The one who said yes when her heart was crying out to say no.

The one who accepted less because she was afraid to hope for more.

That version of me was familiar, and sometimes familiarity feels safer than freedom. I never wanted to be her again, but I remembered her well. I remembered the exhaustion that came from constantly managing other people's expectations. I remembered the anxiety that simmered beneath the surface, always waiting to be triggered by one wrong word or one look of disapproval. I remembered the ache of never feeling like I was enough. And I remembered how easy it had been to disappear into that version of myself, simply because it was all I had ever known.

The fear of going back was not about doubting God. It was about doubting myself. I knew God had begun a new thing in me. I could feel it in the way I responded to situations differently, in the boundaries I began to set, in the peace I carried. But some days, when I felt weak or tired or stretched too thin, I could feel the pull of the past tugging at me. Old patterns do not die quietly. They wait for a moment of vulnerability, then try to reassert themselves.

There were times when I caught myself falling into old ways of thinking. When I felt the need to explain myself to someone who had already made up their mind. When I softened my no into a maybe because I was afraid of disappointing someone. When I bit my tongue because I did not want to be misunderstood. In those moments, I felt the tug of the old me, the one who used to make herself small to be accepted. I felt her hesitation. Her need to please. Her fear of rejection.

But instead of shaming myself for those moments, I began to pause. I began to breathe. I began to speak the truth over my heart. I reminded myself that the past was not my home anymore. I could visit it for understanding, for reflection, even for healing, but I no longer had to live there.

I had moved forward.

I had grown.

I had changed.

And while change did not erase the past, it had given me the power to choose a new response.

There is a tenderness that comes with transformation. You start to see the old version of yourself not as a failure, but as someone who was doing the best she could with what she had. I no longer hated her. I honored her. She was the one who survived. She carried me through some of the hardest chapters of my life. But she was never meant to be the final version of me. She was only the beginning.

Healing is not a straight line. It is not a switch you flip. It is a daily decision. And some days, the fear of going back will feel stronger than your belief in moving forward. On those days, you must return to the truth. You must go back to what God has said about you. You must remember how far you have come. And you must make the decision, again and again, to choose growth over comfort, truth over lies, and freedom over fear.

I learned to identify the triggers that tried to pull me backward. Stress, fatigue, conflict, rejection. Those were the moments when the old patterns would whisper their familiar scripts. Stay quiet. Do not make waves. Say yes and be nice. Do not be too much.

But instead of reacting the way I used to, I began to pause. I began to ask myself what I truly needed. I began to listen to my spirit rather than my fear. I began to trust that the new foundation God was building in me was stronger than the pull of my past.

I stopped trying to prove I had healed by pretending I was never tempted to return to old habits. Healing is not pretending. It is recognizing the temptation to go back and choosing not to. It is standing at the fork in the road and choosing the harder path because it leads to life. It is giving yourself grace when you falter and strength when you rise again.

Every time I chose not to go back, I got a little stronger. Every time I used my voice, every time I honored my boundaries, every time I refused to betray myself for the comfort of others, I was rewriting the story. I was reclaiming my power. I was showing up as the woman I had prayed to become. And each of those moments became a brick in the foundation of my healing.

There were still nights when fear came knocking. When I lay in bed wondering if I would ever be fully free from the shadows of my past. But even then, I knew something had changed. Because I no longer responded to that fear with shame. I responded with the truth.

I reminded myself that healing is not about never being afraid. It is about knowing what to do with that fear when it comes. It is about remembering that God is still with me in every uncertain moment. That His grace still covers me when I fall. That His strength is made perfect in my weakness.

I no longer live with the fear of going back ruling my life. It still whispers sometimes, but it no longer holds power over me. Because I have tasted what it means to be free. And I have decided that freedom is worth protecting. I know now that I can live differently. I can choose differently. I can move forward, even when I feel the past tugging at my heels.

The fear of going back is real, but it is not the final word. It may visit, but it does not get to stay. Because I am no longer that woman who had to hide to survive. I am no longer the girl who thought love had to be earned. I am no longer the version of myself who settled for less because she did not believe she was worth more.

I am walking in healing.

I am walking in truth.

I am walking in grace.

And even on the days when I stumble, I know I will rise again. Because forward is not just a direction. It is a decision.

And I have already decided that I will not go back.

Choosing Forward Every Day

Healing is not a one-time event. It is not something you cross off your list once and for all. It is not a box you check or a place you arrive at and never have to revisit. Healing is a journey. It is a series of choices made one day, one moment, one breath at a time. Some days it feels effortless, like grace is flowing freely through your body. Other days it feels like a battle, like you are fighting against every lie that ever tried to root itself in your soul. But even on the hardest days, healing is still a choice. And it is still worth it.

I used to think there would come a day when I would wake up and just feel healed. I imagined a finish line where all the pain would be gone, all the questions answered, and all the wounds fully closed. But I have come to understand that healing is not linear. It moves like the tide. Some days it crashes against the shore with force and clarity. Other days it gently recedes, asking you to be still and trust what you cannot yet see.

Every day, I must choose to move forward. I must choose to believe that the work God has begun in me is worth continuing, even when I feel tired or uncertain. I must choose to speak truth over my mind when old thoughts try to take root again. I must choose to honor the boundaries that protect my peace, even when others do not understand them. I must choose to show up as the healed version of myself, even when the unhealed parts still cry out for attention.

Some days, choosing forward looks like saying no to things that once made me feel valuable. The people-pleasing. The performance. The constant need to be needed.

Other days, it looks like saying yes to rest, to joy, to solitude, to stillness. Choosing forward means learning that progress is not always loud. Sometimes it is found in the quiet decisions that no one sees. The choice to forgive. The decision to breathe before reacting. The courage to let something go. The strength to keep going when it would be easier to give up.

There are days when I still feel the weight of the past. When the enemy of my soul tries to remind me of who I used to be. When shame knocks on the door and tries to convince me that I have not really changed. On those days, I turn my heart toward God. I remind myself that I am not walking this path alone. That healing was never about me doing everything perfectly. It was always about walking in partnership with the One who knows me completely and loves me fully.

God never asked me to heal myself. He asked me to surrender. To let Him lead. To let Him tend to the broken places with gentleness and grace. So, when the lies come, when fear creeps in, when the temptation to retreat rises, I return to truth. I remember that my identity is not in what I have done or failed to do. It is in who He says I am.

Loved.

Chosen.

Whole.

Redeemed.

Choosing forward also means learning how to sit in the tension of healing. There are days when joy and grief live side by side. When I laugh with ease but still carry a tender ache. When I feel strong in one area but still uncertain in another. I have learned to stop seeing those moments as failures.

They are simply part of the process. Healing is not about reaching a place where nothing ever hurts again. It is about becoming someone who knows how to walk through the hurt without losing herself.

Every time I choose forward, I build trust with myself. I prove to the younger version of me that she is safe now. That she no longer has to perform to be accepted. That she no longer has to settle to be loved. That she no longer has to stay silent to be safe. I let her rest. I let her exhale. I let her become.

There is something sacred about choosing your own healing repeatedly. It is an act of faith. A declaration of worth. A quiet rebellion against the forces that once tried to convince you that you were broken beyond repair. When I choose forward, I am not just deciding for myself. I am making a statement to every lie that ever tried to destroy me. I am saying I will not go back. I am saying I believe in the woman I am becoming.

Choosing forward also means being honest about where I still struggle. It means not pretending I have it all together. It means reaching out for help when I need it. Letting others in. Letting God in. It means trusting that I do not have to be perfect to be progressing. That I can be both healing and whole. Both growing and grounded. Both tender and strong.

Some days, choosing forward looks like writing down a scripture and repeating it until it sinks into my bones. Other days, it looks like crying in the presence of God, knowing He sees every tear and holds every piece of my heart. It looks like choosing to rest when I want to push through. It looks like choosing joy when sorrow still lingers in the background. It looks like holding space for hope, even when I am not sure what the future holds.

There is no formula for healing. No three-step plan that guarantees wholeness. There is only faith. There is only surrender. There is only the daily, moment-by-moment choice to believe that God is doing something beautiful amid the mess. That the woman I am becoming is worth showing up for.

Now, I wake up and remind myself that today is another opportunity. Another step. Another chance to choose the truth. To choose grace. To choose forward. I do not have to have it all figured out. I do not have to rush the process. I simply must keep going. To keep breathing. To keep choosing the life that is unfolding in front of me.

I am not who I used to be. I am not stuck in the places that once held me captive. I am not defined by the pain that shaped me. I am defined by the God who rescued me. And He is still writing my story.

So, I choose forward. Again, and again. Not because it is always easy, but because it is always worth it. Because every step I take is a step away from who I was and a step closer to who I am becoming.

A woman of faith.

A woman of courage.

A woman of peace.

A woman who chooses healing every single day.

She Begins Here

Becoming me was not about achieving perfection or becoming someone new. It was about finally coming home to the woman I had always been beneath the layers of fear, silence, and performance. The confidence I carry now is not about being loud or having all the answers. It is about knowing who I am in God, trusting His voice over the noise, and walking forward even when the path feels uncertain.

This healing journey has taught me that confidence does not begin with applause. It begins in the quiet decisions to show up, speak truth, and honor what God is restoring. It is found in the gentle strength of boundaries, the courage to protect your peace, and the grace to keep choosing forward when the past tries to pull you back.

You do not have to wait until you feel ready to step into who you are becoming. You only must begin. One small step at a time. One surrendered moment at a time.

There is a place ahead where you do not have to pretend anymore, where truth is met with safety, and healing is allowed to begin.

Signs You Are Being Invited Deeper

Many people expect healing to feel like peace right away. But often, the first sign of healing is not peace. It is readiness. Readiness to stop hiding. Readiness to tell the truth. Readiness to face what you once avoided because survival no longer feels like enough.

You may notice that you are more uncomfortable with silence than before. That old excuses no longer soothe you. That the ache you once buried now asks for a voice. This is not regression. This is healing asking for your participation. It is your soul signaling that it is time to move from understanding into truth.

If you feel a quiet pull toward honesty, even when you do not know what it will cost you, that is healing. If you feel a stirring that says, something has to change, even though you do not know how yet, that is healing. Healing does not always come with certainty. Sometimes it comes with a brave willingness to begin. And that willingness is enough.

CHAPTER 6

YOU CAN'T HEAL WHAT YOU WON'T REVEAL

You Are Safe Here

There is something profoundly sacred about the moment we stop pretending. It is not flashy. It is not loud. It rarely comes with applause or celebration. But it is holy. It is that souldeep surrender where we remove the mask and whisper, "I can't keep hiding this anymore." It is the moment when we dare to sit still long enough to feel what we have been out running for years. When we stop silencing the ache and begin to hold space for it, just as it is, without trying to package it for someone else's comfort.

This is not easy. It will likely feel unfamiliar. It may stir discomfort that you cannot fully name. You might even feel like you are breaking apart when you are just beginning to come home to yourself. That lump rising in your throat, that tightness in your chest, that restlessness in your spirit is not a weakness. It is your body, your soul, your whole being responding to truth. It is the deep knowing that you are stepping into something sacred. You are entering holy ground, not because you have it all together, but because you are willing to tell the truth about where you are and what still hurts.

I want you to hear this as clearly as possible: you are safe here. Not because healing is easy or tidy. Not because the road ahead will be smooth. But because this is where God meets us. Not in our polished performance, but in our raw honesty. Not in our strength, but in our surrender. This is the place where the soil of your soul becomes fertile ground for transformation. This is where chains begin to fall and lies begin to unravel. This is where you stop striving and start receiving.

By the time you have reached this part of your journey, you have already walked through valleys that most people will never see. You have faced the darkness with trembling hands. You have chosen to keep reading, to keep showing up, even when your heart whispered that it would be easier to turn away. That matters. That means something. That is evidence of a resilience in you that cannot be undone. It is not just willpower. It is the Spirit of God already breathing new life into places that once felt desolate.

But now, the invitation goes deeper. This next stretch of your journey is not just about reflection. It is about revelation. Not the kind that comes from collecting information or reading more books, but the kind that requires you to dig. To uncover. To lift the veil from parts of your story you have tried to forget. This is where you name what still bleeds. This is where you tell the truth, even if your voice shakes. This is where you stop performing healing and start living it.

Let me tell you something tender and true: it is far easier to talk about healing than to do it. To sit with your pain takes courage most people never tap into. To revisit the places, you swore you had buried for good takes an audacity that can only be described as holy. So many stay stuck because it is simply too painful to open that door. They build a life around the wound. They decorate the exterior, convince themselves they have moved on, but inside, there is still a little girl crying in the dark, asking if anyone will ever come. You cannot keep her waiting any longer.

You cannot walk in freedom if you are still clinging to secrecy. You cannot receive the fullness of restoration while guarding the very places that need to be restored. There is no shortcut around this. There is no formula. There is only the invitation to be honest. To get real. To let the light in.

You cannot heal what you do not reveal.

Many of us were taught to keep going no matter what. To smile through the ache. To never let them see you sweat. We learned early on how to carry the weight of others while ignoring our own. We performed. We perfected. We played roles so well that we even forgot who we were underneath them. But deep down, beneath all the effort and excellence, we knew. We knew something was still broken. Still aching. Still waiting for a place to be seen and soothed.

I lived there for years. I sang the songs. Quoted the verses. Did all the right things while secretly wondering why I still felt empty. Why did the ache linger? Why the joy felt out of reach. I did not know it then, but I was living in a silent war between who I wanted to be and what I was still afraid to face. And no matter how hard I tried to outrun it, the pain kept calling me back. Not to harm me, but to heal me. Not to shame me, but to set me free.

Freedom is not found in hiding. It is found in truth. And truth requires courage.

That is why I want you to stay with me in this chapter. Even if your heart races. Even if you feel exposed. Even if a part of you wants to skim through these pages and move on to something easier. Stay. Sit with it. Let the Spirit of God do what only He can do. He is not here to demand. He is here to dwell. He is not here to rush you. He is here to walk with you. Slowly. Tenderly. Faithfully.

You do not need to open every wound today. But you do need to begin. You do need to let the mask slip. You do need to acknowledge the ache, the grief, the story behind your silence. You need to say it, even if it is just in a whisper: "That still hurts. I still carry that. I have not let that go." Because the truth is, God already knows. He was there. He saw it all. And His love has not wavered for a single second.

There is nothing you have to hide from Him. Not your pain. Not your anger. Not your confusion. Not your questions. He is not asking you to clean yourself up before you come. He is asking you to come. Period. With everything you carry. With all the messy, unsorted, jagged pieces. Because those are the very places He longs to touch. To hold. To heal. This chapter is not about rushing to the breakthrough. It is about honoring the breaking. It is about recognizing that the breaking is sacred. That your pain has a voice. That your story has weight. That your wounds are worthy of gentleness and grace.

You are safe here. Because God is here. And wherever He is, healing is possible. Not because you are strong enough. But because He is tender enough. Loving enough. Present enough.

So, just breathe beautiful. Let this moment mark a shift. You do not need to carry the burden alone anymore. You do not need to pretend that you are fine. You are allowed to be exactly as you are brave, broken, beautiful, becoming.

You are safe here.

And this is where healing begins.

The Heavy Cost of Hiding

There is a high price we pay when we choose to hide our pain. It is often invisible at first. It does not make itself obvious right away. But slowly, quietly, it begins to wear away at our peace. It chips at our sense of self. It steals moments of joy, connection, and truth. And eventually, if we keep hiding long enough, we forget what it feels like to live fully alive.

So many of us were never taught what to do with pain. We were taught to push through, to stay quiet, to keep it together. We were handed masks and told they were strength. We were handed silence and told it was maturity. We were handed denial and told it was faith. So, we learned to survive instead of healing. We learned to function instead of feeling.

We became masters of disguise. We showed up with smiles even when we were unraveling. We offered help to others even when we were falling apart inside. We kept going, kept achieving, kept moving so that no one would look too closely and see the truth. The truth that we were carrying wounds that had not been acknowledged, let alone tended to.

But here is the thing about pain. It will not stay hidden forever. Even when buried deep, it finds its way to the surface. It shows up in anxiety that will not go away. In anger that flares without warning. In a low-grade sadness that lingers, even in happy moments. It shows up in the way we struggle to trust. In the way we pull back from people. In the way we live half-present, half-guarded, always holding something back.

The cost of hiding is not just emotional. It is relational. It touches everything. It keeps us from intimacy, from vulnerability, from joy. It convinces us that being loved requires being perfect. It tells us that our mess is too much, our truth too heavy, our brokenness too ugly to be seen. So, we keep the walls up. We keep the wounds buried. And we wonder why we still feel so alone.

I know what that life feels like. I know the exhaustion of holding it all in. I know the ache of wanting to be known but fearing that the truth will drive people away. I know the hollow feeling of showing up for everyone else while silently praying that someone will notice you are not okay. I know what it means to live with a fractured heart and call it strength.

But hiding never leads to healing. It leads to disconnection. It leads to burnout. It leads to a version of yourself that is a shell, not a soul. And eventually, something breaks. Maybe it is your health. Maybe it is a relationship. Maybe it is your sense of purpose. Whatever it is, it will crumble under the weight of what you were never meant to carry alone.

God never asked you to hide. He never called you to pretend. He never told you to bury your pain and just keep going. In fact, He invites you to do the opposite. He invites you to bring it all to Him. The sorrow. The anger. The confusion. The ache. He is not surprised by your story. He is not offended by your truth. He is not burdened by your tears. He is the one who collects every single one and holds them as sacred.

There is a moment in every healing journey when you must decide that hiding is no longer an option. That pretending is no longer sustainable. That surviving is not enough. That you want to be free more than you want to be comfortable. That you want to live fully more than you want to appear fine.

It is the moment when you stop negotiating with your pain and start facing it. When you stop making excuses for your silence and start naming what has been buried. When you stop shrinking to protect others and start honoring the truth of your own soul.

Yes, it is scary. Yes, it may feel like it was too much at first. But it is not more than God can handle. It is not more than His grace can cover. And it is not more than your spirit can survive. You were created for wholeness. And wholeness begins with truth.

There is power in naming your pain. Power in saying, this happened. It mattered. And I am allowed to feel what I feel about it. You do not need anyone's permission to speak your truth. You do not need anyone to validate your pain for it to be real. You do not need the approval of those who hurt you before you begin to heal from what they did.

You only need to be honest.

Jesus said, you will know the truth, and the truth will set you free. That freedom begins with your willingness to stop hiding. To stop minimizing. To stop carrying it all alone. Because healing does not begin when you get over the pain.

Healing begins when you finally turn and face it.

Avoidance will not save you. Performance will not sustain you. Numbness will not protect you. Only truth can set you free. Only honesty can create space for healing to begin. And you are allowed to be honest.

You are allowed to admit that you are tired. That you are hurting. That something still lingers from your past. That a part of you is still waiting for closure. You are allowed to admit that you have wounds that are not visible but are just as real. You are allowed to say you need healing, even if your life looks functional from the outside.

God is not calling you to fake it. He is calling you to freedom.

And freedom begins when you choose to stop hiding. When you choose to trust that what is revealed in the light will not destroy you but will deliver you.

This is your invitation to come out of hiding. To lay it down. To tell the truth. Not for the sake of rehashing the past, but for the sake of finally releasing its grip on your present.

There is nothing too heavy for the heart of God. Nothing too dark for His light. Nothing too broken for His hands.

You do not have to carry this anymore.

Let today be the day you stop hiding and begin to heal.

Shame does not get the final word.

If hiding is the barrier to healing, then shame is the voice guarding the door. It lurks in the background of our lives, disguised as protection but working hard to keep us isolated. Shame convinces us that silence is safer. That vulnerability is too risky. That truth will cost us more than it will heal. It whispers that if we dare to speak about what hurts us, we will lose love, respect, connection, and belonging.

But shame is a liar.

Shame does not speak the truth. It speaks of fear. It builds walls instead of bridges. It chains you to your past and calls it your identity. It turns moments of brokenness into permanent labels and then dares you to defy them. Shame tells you that what happened to you was your fault. That you should be over it by now. That if people really knew what you carried, they would pull away. That if God knew the details, He would disqualify you.

But those are lies. All of them.

The truth is that God already knows. He saw the moment the pain entered your life. He witnessed every betrayal, every rejection, every silent tear, every internal war you fought alone. And not once did He turn away. Not once did He step back in disgust or disapproval. He leaned closer. With compassion. With tenderness. With grace.

Shame wants you to believe that your story disqualifies you. That your mistakes define you. That your brokenness makes you unworthy. But God says something different. He says you are chosen. He says you are whole. He says you are made in His image and that nothing about your past can undo your identity in Him.

Shame does not just attach itself to what happened. It attaches itself to how we see ourselves because of what happened. It says you are not just someone who went through something hard. It says you are damaged. It says you are unlovable. It says you are too much. Or not enough. It says your worth has an expiration date, and you missed it.

And if you have carried shame for a long time, you know how convincing it can be. It sounds so familiar that you stop questioning it. You start believing that it is just the truth. That you deserve to carry this weight. That maybe this is just who you are now.

But you are not your shame.

You are not your worst day. You are not the thing that happened to you. You are not the decision you regret. You are not the silence you kept for years. You are not what they called you in anger or neglect. You are not the identity shame handed you when you were at your lowest.

You are loved.

You are seen.

You are chosen.

You are still becoming the woman God had in mind when He first thought of you. The one who would rise from ashes. The one who would walk through fire and still carry grace. The one who would take the shattered pieces of her story and place them in the hands of a God who redeems all things.

Shame wants you to keep quiet. But healing asks you to speak. Not to everyone. Not recklessly. But intentionally. First to yourself. Then to God. And maybe, when you are ready, to safe and trusted people who can remind you of your worth when you forget.

There is something powerful that happens when you say the words out loud. When you take what shame told you to bury and you bring it into the light. Its grip begins to loosen. Its voice begins to fade. And in its place, truth begins to rise.

You begin to see that you are not disqualified. You are being refined.

You begin to understand that what the enemy meant for evil, God is using for good.

You begin to believe that you can be both wounded and worthy. That you can hold sorrow and still carry hope. That you can be in process and still be powerful.

There is no shame that grace cannot cover. No wound too deep for the love of God. He is not waiting for you to clean yourself up. He is not asking for perfection. He is asking for honesty. For surrender. For trust.

When Jesus went to the cross, He did not just carry your sin. He carried your shame. Every hidden moment. Every false identity. Every heavy lie. It was all placed on

Him. And when He declared, it is finished, He meant it. Shame lost its power in that moment. But it is up to you to stop agreeing with it. It is up to you to lay it down.

Because shame may have had a loud voice in your past, but it does not get to have the final word in your future.

Only God gets that.

And His word over you is love. His word is healing. His word is freedom.

So, what would it look like to live as if shame no longer owned your story?

What would it look like to wake up and believe that you are already enough?

What would it feel like to breathe without the weight of pretending?

That is what healing invites you into. A life where you are no longer defined by what hurt you, but by the One who heals you.

Let shame fall silent.

Let truth rise loudly.

Let grace take up space.

You do not have to live under the weight of what was.

You are allowed to walk forward in what is.

And what is true now is this:

You are free.

You are whole.

You are loved.

You are not too much.

You are not too far gone.

You are enough.

Let that truth be louder than the lies.

Let that truth become the new foundation beneath your feet. And every time shame tries to speak, let grace speak louder.

What Healing Really Feels Like

Healing is not neat. It is not tidy or predictable. It does not come in a perfectly wrapped package with clear instructions and a guaranteed timeline. Healing is messy. It is tender. It is often inconvenient. And yet, it is one of the most sacred things you will ever experience.

We often expect healing to feel like triumph. We imagine ourselves waking up one day, completely free from the weight of our pain. We want the process to be quick and clean. We want to feel strong every step of the way. But healing rarely looks or feels that way. Sometimes, it feels like unraveling. Like letting go of everything you thought you had to hold together to finally make room for truth.

Sometimes healing feels like peace, and other times it feels like grief. Sometimes it feels like joy rising in your chest for the first time in years. Other times, it feels like a deep ache surfacing when you least expect it. There are days when healing brings laughter, and there are days when it invites tears. Both are holy. Both are welcome.

Healing does not mean forgetting. It does not mean pretending something never happened. It means remembering differently. It means seeing the pain through the lens of grace instead of shame. It means no longer letting the past have the final say. It means choosing to believe that even what hurt you can be used to grow you.

There will be moments when you feel like you are taking three steps forward and two steps back. That does not mean you are failing. That means you are human. That means you are in process. That means you are doing the hard work of becoming. Growth is not always visible. Sometimes the biggest healing happens in silence. In rest. In simply choosing not to give up.

Healing may look like setting boundaries that feel uncomfortable at first. It may sound like saying no without guilt. It may feel like finally telling the truth out loud and letting the weight of secrecy fall away. It may mean choosing rest over hustle. It may mean asking for help, admitting you are not okay, and letting someone sit with you in sorrow.

Sometimes healing means revisiting old wounds that you thought were closed. It means noticing how certain situations still trigger a reaction in you. It means giving yourself grace when you do not respond perfectly. It means acknowledging that growth is not about never hurting again. It is about learning how to respond with compassion instead of criticism. With presence instead of avoidance. With truth instead of shame.

Healing may bring clarity. It may help you see your story with new eyes. But it may also bring questions. It may stir up things you were not prepared to face. That is not a setback. That is part of the work. It is your soul inviting you to go deeper. Not to hurt more, but to heal more honestly.

There is no shame in taking your time. There is no prize for rushing through your pain. You are allowed to move slowly. You are allowed to pause. You are allowed to hold joy in one hand and sorrow in the other. Healing often happens in those in-between places. In the tension of feeling both broken and whole. Of holding grief and hope at the same time.

Some days you may feel like a completely different person. Other days you may feel like the old version of yourself is still lurking in the corners of your mind. That is normal. That is the rhythm of healing. It is not a straight road. It is a winding path with detours and delays. But every step matters. Even the ones that feel small. Especially the ones that feel small.

Healing may look like forgiving someone who never apologized. It may mean releasing the need to be understood. It may mean letting go of expectations you once placed on yourself or others. It may look like creating space for new dreams. For new relationships. For a new way of being.

It may not be loud. It may not be visible to others. But you will feel it. In the way your shoulders begin to relax. In the way your breathing slows. In the way you no longer feel the need to explain your existence. In the way you begin to trust your own voice again.

Healing is often quiet. It does not always make an entrance. Sometimes it comes in the form of one small decision. One boundary honored. One hard truth faced.

One deep breath taken when anxiety says you cannot. It comes in the choice to stay. To sit. To feel. To not run this time.

And when you look back, you may be surprised at how far you have come. Not because everything is perfect, but because you are different. You are softer in the places you used to be guarded. You are stronger in the places you once felt weak. You are wiser in the spaces that used to confuse you. You are more anchored than you have ever been.

That is healing. Not perfection. Not performance. But presence. Honesty. Grace.

Healing is remembering who you are. Who you have always been. Who God has called you to be. It is not about fixing yourself. It is about coming home to yourself. To the woman underneath the layers of fear, shame, silence, and sorrow. The woman who is still here. Still standing. Still becoming.

Let that be enough today. Let it be enough that you are choosing to show up for your own healing. Let it be enough that you are willing to feel what you used to numb. Let it be enough that you are still here, still open, still willing to grow.

Healing is not something you earn. It is something you receive. And it is already happening. Even now. Even here. Even in you.

CHAPTER 7

LEARNING TO WALK WHILE STILL LIMPING

The Fragile First Steps

There is a particular tenderness that surrounds the beginning of a new chapter in your healing. It is not the kind of beginning that announces itself loudly. It does not arrive with fanfare or applause. Instead, it unfolds quietly, almost imperceptibly. It shows up in a small decision, like choosing to get out of bed when everything in you wants to stay under the covers.

It whispers in the choice to respond to God with just a single word: "Okay." It begins in the sacred silence between who you were and who you are becoming. These are not the beginnings the world often sees or celebrates, but heaven leans in close for these moments. Because they are not small to God. They are holy.

After a season or even a lifetime of survival, beginning again can feel like betrayal. Not of others, but of yourself. The version of you who endured, who carried the weight, who kept everyone else steady while she was unraveling in secret. That version of you worked hard to protect you. She built walls when safety was scarce. She numbed the pain when feeling it would have crushed you. She became everything you needed just to make it through. And now, as healing begins to stir within you, it can feel like you are leaving her behind. But you are not betraying her. You are honoring her. You are telling her, "You did well. You got us this far. But now, it is time to rest. It is time to heal."

These first steps into healing are often misunderstood. You are not walking strong. You are walking tender. You are not sprinting toward wholeness. You are inching forward, often with tears in your eyes and a tremble in your voice. You may feel exposed. Unsure. Unsteady. And that is completely normal. Healing rarely begins with certainty. It usually begins with a risk, a risk of believing that there is more for you than just surviving. A risk to believe that healing is not just for other people, but for you, too.

You may find yourself pausing often, looking back at where you came from, not because you want to return, but because the past shaped so much of who you are. And now, without the old patterns to lean on, without the familiar coping mechanisms, you feel disoriented. This is what growth feels like. It is the disorientation that comes when you have decided to step out of the shadows and into the light. Your heart is raw. Your emotions are heightened. You feel everything. And for someone who has learned to feel nothing for so long, that alone can be overwhelming.

This liminal space, the space between brokenness and full restoration, is where your most sacred work will take place. It is the space where you stop measuring your healing by how quickly you move and start measuring it by how present you are. It is where God meets you with a gentleness you may have never known. He is not pushing you to rush.

He is not waiting with a clipboard to evaluate your progress. He is walking beside you, matching your pace, whispering, "I'm proud of you," every time you choose to keep going, even when your steps are slow and your confidence is fragile.

There will be days when hope feels far away. When you wake up and feel like you have regressed. When the weight of what you have lost feels heavier than the hope of what you are building. On those days, I want you to remember that the mere fact that you are still choosing to show up is a miracle. The fact that you are still standing limping, maybe, but standing is sacred. You do not need to be perfect to be powerful. You do not need to be finished to be faithful. You do not need to be healed to be whole in the eyes of God.

These fragile first steps are where your faith will deepen. Not because everything suddenly makes sense, but because you are learning to trust God in real time. You are learning to lean into grace when the ground beneath your feet still feels unfamiliar. You are learning to listen to your soul, to give it permission to breathe, to rest, to cry, to hope again. That kind of learning is slow. But it is transformational.

You may not realize it, but every time you choose to keep walking, you are rewriting your story. You are teaching your body and your spirit a new rhythm, one that is no longer led by trauma, but by truth. You are disrupting old narratives that told you had to be strong all the time.

You are laying down shame that said you had to have it all figured out. And in its place, you are picking up compassion, mercy, and softness. Not weakness. Softness—the kind of strength that does not harden to survive but opens to heal.

There is no wrong way to begin again. Maybe your first step is making a phone call. Maybe it is opening your Bible after months of silence. Maybe it is allowing yourself to be quiet without guilt. Maybe it is asking for help. Maybe it is praying, "God, I don't know what I'm doing, but I want to follow You." Every one of those steps counts.

Your limp is not something to hide. It is a sign that you are moving forward. It is the evidence of your survival. It is your declaration that though life tried to take you out, you are still here. And you are still becoming. The world may overlook this season. It may not applaud your slow progress or understand your quiet courage. But heaven sees it all. Heaven sees you.

So, take another step, no matter how unsteady. Let yourself begin, again and again, as many times as you need. You are not late. You are not behind. You are on holy ground. You are walking with the One who knows every scar, every fear, every trembling step and loves you through it all.

This is the beginning. And it is more than enough.

The Ache of Remembering

There is an ache that often rises not at the beginning of our pain, but in the middle of our healing. It surprises many of us. We assume that once we start moving forward, the past will loosen its grip. That the act of choosing healing will somehow mute the memories that once held us captive. But the truth is, healing has a way of bringing things to the surface. It has a way of waking up the parts of us we had to numb to survive. And when those parts begin to stir, they often bring memories with them memories we thought we had buried deep enough to forget.

The ache of remembering is not just about the events themselves. It is about what they cost us. It is about the pieces of ourselves that we lost along the way. We silenced the laughter. The innocence that was stolen. The dreams that were abandoned out of necessity, not choice. It is the sting of realizing how young you were when you were forced to grow up. How alone you felt when you needed someone to notice. How much you carried that was never meant to be yours. It is grief, not only for what happened, but for what did not. For the love you longed for and never received. For safety you needed and never had. For the apology that never came. For the closure that still feels out of reach.

Remembering can feel like regression, but it is not. It is a revelation. It is the Spirit of God gently shining light on the places still aching in silence. And while the ache may feel unbearable, it is a sign that you are becoming more whole, not less. Because what once lived in darkness is now being seen. And what is seen can finally be soothed.

These memories do not come to destroy you. They come to be healed. They come as invitations to truth, to compassion, to deeper restoration. And yet, when they rise, they often carry weight. Sometimes the ache is sudden and sharp, brought on by a smell, a song, a phrase that takes you back to a moment you thought you had forgotten. Other times, it is a slow dull ache that settles in your chest and makes you feel heavy for days. It is not always logical. It does not always follow a pattern. But it is always real. And it is always worth paying attention to.

You may question your progress when these memories resurface. You may feel like you have taken ten steps back. But the presence of grief does not mean the absence of growth. In fact, it often means the opposite. Because you are now strong enough to face what you could not before. You are now resourced with truth, with support, with faith, with grace. You are no longer that child who had to endure it alone. You are an adult who is learning to honor her past without being defined by it.

And in this remembering, you will grieve. Not just the events, but the person you had to become to survive them. You may grieve the years you spent pretending. The relationships that were lost because you could not be honest yet. The faith that cracked under the weight of unanswered prayers. The self-worth that eroded slowly under the pressure to be strong. You may grieve who you could have been if the trauma had not written parts of your story. That grief is valid. That grief is holy.

Let yourself feel the sorrow that remembering brings. Cry if you need to. Rage if you must. Sit in silence if words feel too small. But do not shut it down. Do not numb it away. Do not rush past it. The ache of remembering is not meant to last forever, but it must be allowed to pass through. It is a wave that needs to crest before it can recede. And on the other side of that wave is something sacred. A deeper understanding of yourself. A deeper intimacy with God. A deeper compassion for your journey.

God is not afraid of your memories. He does not turn away when they rise. He draws nearer. He sits with you in the remembering. He weeps with you over what was lost. He grieves the pain you endured. And He does not try to explain it away. He simply stays. And slowly, as you invite Him into those places, healing begins to write a new story not by erasing the past, but by redeeming it.

This is what God does. He takes the very things that once threatened to destroy us and turns them into sacred markers of His mercy. Not all memories will be softened right away. Some may still sting. But over time, as grace continues its work, the sharpness begins to dull. The weight begins to lift. And what once triggered shame now becomes a testimony of survival.

You may never fully understand why some things happened the way they did. You may never get the apology you deserve. You may never be able to make sense of it all. But healing does not require perfect understanding. It requires presence. And your presence in this process is enough. God's presence in your pain is enough. Together, you are rewriting what once broke you.

So let the ache come. Let it wash over you. Let it remind you of how far you have already come. Let it teach you that healing is not a straight line, but a series of sacred pauses, holy remembering, and brave forward steps. You are allowed to feel it all. You are allowed to hold space for the pain while still holding on to hope.

The past shaped you, but it does not own you. The memories may arise, but they do not get to rule. The ache may linger, but it no longer defines your identity. You are more than what happened to you. You are a woman who remembers, who grieves, who heals, who rises. And the ache? It is only a sign that you are alive, awake, and in the process of becoming whole.

The Courage to Keep Showing Up

There is a kind of courage that does not look like strength. It does not roar. It does not march confidently into battle. It does not make headlines or win applause. It is quieter. Quieter, but no less powerful. It is the kind of courage that rises when everything in you wants to stay down. It is the kind of courage that chooses to keep showing up when every voice in your mind tells you to quit. It is the courage to live in the tension between healing and hurting, between hope and heartbreak, between what you are letting go of and what you have not yet grasped.

Some days, this courage looks like rising out of bed with heavy limbs and a heavier heart. Other days, it looks like keeping your appointment with your therapist even though every part of you wants to cancel. Sometimes it is answering a text message from someone who cares when you would rather withdraw. Sometimes it is letting someone pray for you even when you feel numb. Sometimes it is simply breathing deep, slowly, intentionally because you are learning to be present in a body and a life that once felt foreign or unsafe.

You may not feel brave. You may not feel strong. You may feel like you are just barely holding it together. But every time you choose to take one small step toward healing, you are doing holy work. Every time you refuse to disappear into your old patterns, you are declaring, "I am still here." Every time you offer your heart to God, even when it is weary or unsure, you are writing a new story with your very breath.

Healing is not linear. There will be days when you feel like you are finally making progress—like something in you has shifted and you can breathe a little easier. And then, without warning, a memory, a song, a dream, or a conversation will pull you back into the ache. You may feel like you are starting over. You may be tempted to believe that the ground you gained was not real. But that is not true. That is the nature of healing. It ebbs and flows. It spirals and circles. You revisit the same places, not because you fail to heal, but because you are healing more deeply than before.

And here is what is beautiful about that: every time you return to a place of pain, you bring with you more awareness, more tools, more grace. You are not the same person who stood there the last time. This time, you come with God's truth echoing in your soul. This time, you come with the understanding that you are not alone. This time, you come with the ability to name what you feel and hold space for it. That is not going backward. That is becoming.

Showing up does not always mean doing something big. Sometimes it means resting. Sometimes it means crying. Sometimes it means sitting in stillness and letting your heart be held. God is not measuring your effort by how visible your progress is. He sees your private battles. He hears your silent prayers. He knows the weight of every small act of obedience, every yes whispered through tears, every choice to trust Him when nothing makes sense.

Do not underestimate the holy significance of your perseverance. Do not minimize the victory of continuing to hope when despair is easier. You are doing sacred work. You are moving through pain, not around it. You are staying in the process when leaving would feel more comfortable. That is the kind of strength that heaven celebrates. That is the kind of faith that moves mountains, even if it begins with the size of a mustard seed.

There may be people around you who do not understand your journey. They may wonder why you are still struggling. They may not know how to hold space for your healing. That is okay. They do not have to understand for your progress to be valid. What matters most is that you and God are walking this road together. And He understands every step. Every stumble. Every moment you show up in brokenness and still choose to believe that something new is being born.

Sometimes showing up looks like worship through tears. Sometimes it is praying with clenched fists and a trembling voice. Sometimes it is journaling when you do not know what to say. Sometimes it is reading Scripture even when it feels distant. Sometimes it is asking for help. Sometimes it is saying no. Sometimes it is setting boundaries. Sometimes it is simply not quitting. These acts, though small, are powerful. They are seeds. Seeds of hope. Seeds of healing. Seeds of faith.

And every seed matters.

You are braver than you think. Braver than your fear will ever admit. Braver than your past tried to convince you. And every time you show up for your healing, every time you return to the process instead of running from it, you are walking in courage that is deeply rooted in the presence of God.

Keep showing up. Even when it hurts. Even when it is messy. Even when you feel like you are not doing enough. You are enough. You are seen. You are held. You are not walking alone.

Healing Without Arrival

There is an illusion many of us carry into our healing journey, even if we do not realize it. We believe that if we do the work, pray the prayers, cry the tears, and press through the pain, we will eventually reach a moment where everything is finally finished.

A moment when we are fully healed, fully whole, fully unshaken. We imagine a destination where the ache never returns, where triggers are silenced forever, and where joy replaces every shadow without resistance. And we long for it. Not because we are impatient, but because we are tired. So tired. And the idea of arrival feels like rest. It feels like a finish line we desperately want to cross.

But healing does not work that way. Healing is not a place you arrive at once and for all. It is not a straight path with a tidy ending. It is a journey. A rhythm. A process that unfolds layer by layer, year by year, moment by moment. You will have days when you feel light and free and strong. And you will have days when the past still lingers, when grief resurfaces, when anxiety returns. Those moments do not mean you are failing. They mean you are human. They mean you are alive. They mean you are still becoming.

It is not that healing does not happen. It does. Deep, beautiful, transformative healing. You will grow. You will change. You will soften. You will feel stronger than you ever have before.

You will experience moments of breakthrough, where you sense the weight lift and your soul exhale. But even then, you may still carry remnants. Not chains, but scars. Not wounds, but tenderness. And those remnants are not proof that you have not healed. They are proof that you have survived something that mattered. They are evidence that your healing has depth.

You are allowed to feel frustrated when healing feels slow. You are allowed to feel disappointed when the pain rises again without warning. You are allowed to ask God, "Why am I still walking through this?" But do not let those questions convince you that you are behind. You are not late. You are not stuck. You are not broken beyond repair. You are on a journey that does not require arrival to be meaningful.

In the Kingdom of God, arrival is not the goal. Abiding is. Abiding means staying with God through every part of the journey. It means learning to rest in Him even when you do not feel rested. It means letting His presence be enough, even when your circumstances are not. Jesus never promised us that we would reach a moment in this life where all pain would disappear. But He did promise to be with us in it. To walk with us. To carry us when we cannot walk. To hold our hand when the path feels steep and rocky and never-ending.

In John 15, Jesus invites us to abide. To remain. Not to perform. Not to arrive. Not to impress. Just to stay with Him. That invitation is the heartbeat of healing. It is the reminder that you are already loved, already seen, already enough. Right now. In the middle. In the mess. In the not-yet.

You do not have to wait until everything is finished to live freely. You do not have to be completely healed to be used by God. You do not have to reach a place of perfection to walk in purpose. You can live fully right here, with the limp, with the questions, with the parts of you that are still learning how to breathe again. Because grace was never about completion. It was always about connection.

There will be people who try to rush your process. They will expect you to be over it. To move on. To let it go. They may not understand that healing is not a one-time event. It is a sacred unfolding. It is the unlearning of years of survival. It is the rebuilding of trust—in yourself, in others, in God. You do not owe them an explanation. You do not have to defend your pace. The One who formed your heart knows exactly what it needs. And He is not in a hurry.

So, release the pressure to arrive. Let go of the finish line. You are not on a schedule. You are on a journey. And the beauty is not waiting at the end. The beauty is in every brave step you take, every honest prayer you pray, every tear you let fall without shame. The beauty is in your resilience, in your softening, in your becoming.

You are not waiting to be whole. You are already being made whole. Right now. In this moment. Even with the ache.

Especially with the ache. Your limp is not a sign that you missed the mark. It is a sign that you are still walking. That you are still choosing life. That you are still saying yes to healing, even when it costs you everything.

There is no arrival point where you stop needing God. There is no milestone that makes grace unnecessary.

There is no day where your need for Him will be less than it is right now. And that is the good news. Because it means you do not have to carry this alone. You never have. You never will.

You are not unfinished in a shameful way. You are unfinished in a beautiful way. In the way an artist leaves space for more color, more detail, more light. God is not done with you. And He is not frustrated by your progress. He is delighted in your becoming. Every brushstroke of your story is intentional. Every scar is being touched by His healing hand. And every step you take, even the halting ones, are bringing you deeper into the life He created you to live.

So, stop chasing arrival. Start cherishing presence. Because God is in the process. And so are you.

Grace for the Limping Places

There are parts of your story that still ache. Parts of your heart that have not quite caught up with your hope. You are moving forward, yes. You are healing, yes. But there are still places that limp when the past brushes up against the present. And that does not mean you are failing. It means you are human. It means you have lived. It means you are still in process.

We often want our healing to be neat. Clean. Linear. We want to point to a moment and say, "That's the day it was all fixed." But healing is not tidy. It is messy and miraculous. It is both progress and pause. It is both joy and sorrow. There are days when you will laugh with your whole chest, and moments later, cry for the girl you used to be. There are mornings when you will feel free, only to stumble across an old memory in the afternoon and feel your chest tightened again. That is not regression. That is reality.

You are not weak because you still limp. The limp is not a liability. It is a sign that you are walking through what once kept you paralyzed. It is evidence that you have survived. That you are still becoming. That something in you chose life when silence felt safer. That something in you keeps showing up, even when healing feels hard.

The world may try to convince you that limping disqualifies you. That if you were strong, you would walk tall and straight without faltering. But God sees it differently. In His eyes, your limp is not a mark of shame. It is a mark of grace. It is the holy evidence of your endurance. It is the testimony that you did not give up. That you did not let the pain have the final word.

In 2 Corinthians 12, Paul speaks of a thorn in his flesh—something painful that would not go away no matter how much he pleaded with God. And what did God say in response? "My grace is sufficient for you, for my power is made perfect in weakness." Paul's thorn did not vanish. His limp remained. And yet, he found strength in the very place he once saw as weakness. That is the invitation of grace. Not to eliminate every sign of pain, but to transform it into something sacred.

You are not a burden because you still struggle. You are not a failure because some wounds still need tending. You are a living, breathing, walking testimony of resilience. And grace is not waiting for you to get it together. Grace will meet you right here. In this moment. In this limp. In this ongoing story.

Give yourself permission to go slow. To pause when you need to. To cry when the ache returns. To rest without guilt. To say, "I am still healing," and let that be enough. You do not owe anyone an explanation for your pace. You do not have to prove your strength by pushing through. You are allowed to tend to your heart with tenderness. You are allowed to be gentle with yourself.

Grace for the limping places means holding space for the truth that you are both strong and soft. Both capable and vulnerable. Both brave and still becoming. It means recognizing that you are doing the best you can with what you have, and that is more than enough. It means letting go of the expectation that healing should look like perfection. And embracing the truth that healing looks like presence, like progress, like permission to be exactly where you are.

Some people will not understand your limp. They may expect you to walk faster, to "get over it," to be someone you are not ready to be. That is not your burden to carry. You are not responsible for their expectations. You are responsible for your own heart. Your own soul. Your own journey with God. And He is not asking you to walk faster. He is asking you to walk with Him.

When you limp, you lean. You lean into the presence of the One who walks beside you. You lean into grace that does not run out. You lean into mercy that renews every single morning. And in that leaning, you find a strength that is not your own. A strength that holds you steady. A strength that will never let you fall too far or wander too long.

You may never walk without a limp on this side of eternity. But you can still walk in peace. You can still walk in purpose. You can still walk in love. And one day, every scar will tell a story of the God who carried you through what you thought you could not survive.

So, if today you find yourself walking slower than you had hoped, let it be. If your soul still aches when you thought it would be settled, be kind to yourself. If your limp feels obvious, let it be a reminder—not of pain, but of progress. You are walking. You are healing. You are becoming.

Let grace carry you the rest of the way.

Walking Forward with Grace

Healing does not always look like leaping. Sometimes, it looks like limping forward with shaky legs and a tender heart. Sometimes, it looks like it is saying yes to one more day, even when your soul feels tired. It looks like trusting that God is working in you, even when you cannot see the fruit yet. It looks like holding space for your progress, even when your pain resurfaces without warning. Healing, in its truest form, is not defined by how perfect your path looks, but by how faithful your heart remains when the journey gets hard.

You are not meant to hide your limp. You are not meant to cover your scars. These are not flaws to be fixed. They are evidence of where God met you, carried you, and restored you piece by piece. They are proof that you kept walking when life tried to stop you. They are reminders that healing does not erase your past but transforms it into sacred ground.

So, take a deep breath, right here in this moment. Place your hand over your heart and honor the fact that you are still here. Still breathing. Still showing up. Still hoping. Still becoming. Your limp is not the end of your story. It is the beginning of a new way of walking with grace as your pace, and God as your strength.

Be patient with your process. Be kind to the parts of you still learning how to trust again. And remember this: the goal is not to walk without weakness. The goal is to walk in the presence of the One who is strong when you are not. Every step, no matter how small, is seen. Every tremble, every sigh, every whisper of hope is heard. And every day you choose to keep going, you are becoming more of who you were always meant to be.

You are already walking in victory, even if you limp the whole way there.

CHAPTER 8

WHEN THE SOUL BEGINS TO EXHALE

There is a sacred moment in every healing journey when something deep inside finally exhales. It does not always come with fireworks or fanfare. Sometimes, it arrives in the stillness, wrapped in quiet that no one else notices. It comes gently, like the softest wind brushing past your soul.

Maybe you wake up one morning and realize the pain in your chest is not quite as sharp. Maybe you hear yourself laughing and pause because it did not feel forced or hollow. Maybe you find yourself in silence and, for the first time in a long while, you do not feel the urge to escape it. Instead, you feel safe in your own presence.

The ache is still there, but it has softened. The grief has not disappeared, but it no longer chokes every breath.

Something has shifted, however slightly. Something is loosening. Something long held is beginning to let go.

This is the beginning of the exhale.

It does not mean the pain has vanished. Healing is rarely about the immediate disappearance of hurt. More often, it is about learning how to live again in the presence of it. This first exhale means you are beginning to breathe again, not just with your lungs but with your spirit. You are letting go of the belief that you must keep everything together or else everything will fall apart. You are loosening your grip on the guilt that has kept your soul stuck in place. You are no longer gripping the silence that once protected you but now only echoes your isolation. You are no longer surviving in fragments. You are beginning to live whole, even in your brokenness.

This moment, however quiet or unnoticed by others, is a holy invitation. It is the whisper of God calling you to something lighter, something freer, something truer than the mask you've worn. "Come to me, all you who are weary and burdened, and I will give you rest" (Matthew 11:28).

That invitation was not written for the polished or the put together. It was spoken into the lives of the weary, the hurting, the barely-holding-on.

These words are not ancient promises we read like history. They are present truth, alive today, still breathing their hope into your now. Rest is not only for those who finish the race. It is for those who are crawling forward on wounded knees, those who keep showing up even when they are not sure how.

Healing is not always loud. More often, it is soft. It is sacred. It is the slow unraveling of lies and the rebuilding of truth, brick by brick, breath by breath. It does not always feel like progress, but every exhale is proof that something is being released. Every breath that reaches deeper into your being is a declaration that you are no longer chained to what once held you captive. Something is mending.

Something is moving. Something is being born anew.

The Weight You Were Never Meant to Carry

There are burdens we pick up without fully realizing it.

Some are placed on our shoulders in childhood, shaped by words that pierced instead of protected, shaped by betrayals that shattered what little safety we had. Sometimes it is not what was said, but what was not. Silence can be just as heavy as a shouted accusation.

We learn to carry pain early, to absorb blame that was never ours. Abuse wrapped in denial. Rejection masked as tough love. Abandonment buried beneath smiles at the dinner table. Other burdens accumulate over time. They are the invisible expectations, the unspoken rules we feel obligated to follow. Be the strong one. Do not complain. Do not cry. Do not be too much. Do not need anything. We carry it all, believing this is what love looks like. Believing this is what faith requires. But it is not. It never was.

We learn to smile while breaking. We show up while unraveling. We offer our strength while denying our own weakness. And somewhere along the way, we forget how to ask for help. We forget that we were never meant to carry it all. Not the guilt. Not the shame. Not the weight of everyone else's expectations. God did not design us to live like that. He did not create us to be human pack mules, weighed down by the burdens of the world. He created us for relationship, for connection, for grace. Not for performance. Not for perfection. Not for silent suffering.

"You were never meant to carry this alone," God whispers, again and again, into the places where we still feel responsible for things we could never control. Galatians 6:2 calls us to carry each other's burdens, but never to the point of self-destruction. We forget that we are not just burden-bearers for others. We are also the ones who are meant to rest. To release. To be held. Psalm 55:22 reminds us, "Cast your cares on the Lord and He will sustain you." That is sustaining love. A promise that does not shame us for needing help but welcomes us into a deeper strength, His strength.

You were never meant to carry the shame that was not yours. You were not meant to carry the blame for someone else's choices. You were not created to walk around dragging chains of guilt or bitterness that only poison your joy. These things have shaped you, yes, but they are not your identity. They are not your story's end. They are not your truth. You are more than what happened to you. You are more than what they said about you. You are more than what you have believed about yourself.

But when you have carried something heavy for so long, setting it down feels risky. Freedom is unfamiliar. Rest feels unsafe. You have been living under pressure for so long that the idea of peace almost feels uncomfortable. Like walking into a quiet room and not knowing what to do with the silence. But friend, you do not have to keep living like this. You do not have to be the one who always holds everything together. You do not have to be the one who always says "I'm fine" when you are not.

God sees your weariness. He sees the nights you cry in silence. He sees the smile you wear for others and the ache you carry when no one is watching. He is not asking you to keep pretending. He is not asking you to keep pushing. He is inviting you to lay it all down. Not because the pain did not matter. Not because you were not wounded. But because you were never meant to carry it alone.

This kind of surrender is sacred. It is not lazy. It is not passive. It is brave. It is a holy resistance against the lie that you must do it all. It is courage wrapped in a whisper: "God, I cannot do this anymore. Please carry it for me." And He will. He always does. He always has. "Come to me," Jesus says, "and I will give you rest." That is not a metaphor. That is a lifeline.

You do not need to be perfect. You do not need to have eloquent words. You do not need to be strong. You only need to be willing. Willing to stop carrying what was never yours. Willing to let go so that you can finally breathe.

What It Means to Truly Let Go

Letting go is one of the most sacred, terrifying, and liberating parts of healing. It sounds so simple just release what is hurting you. But when what you are holding has become a part of your identity, the act of loosening your grip can feel like losing yourself. Pain, after all, is familiar. It is what we have known.

Bitterness, regret, anger, grief, they have become companions in the dark. We hold them not because we love them, but because we have built our lives around them. We have structured our choices, our relationships, our inner dialogue around what hurt us. And when you are finally asked to let go, it can feel like being asked to cut off a part of yourself.

For many of us, the things we are being asked to release once helped us survive. That bitterness? It kept us from trusting people who would have hurt us more. That control? It was our safety net in a world that felt unpredictable. That anger? It was our shield against vulnerability.

Letting go of those things feels like laying down in the middle of a battlefield without armor. It feels like standing in the open and saying, "I trust You to protect me now." And that level of trust feels like too much when your heart has been broken.

But letting go is not weakness. It is strength. It is the quiet, trembling kind of strength that no one sees but God.

It is not loud or proud or public. It is the strength of open hands, of a whispered prayer that says, "I can't carry this anymore." Letting go is not about denying the pain or pretending the past did not happen. It is about saying, "I refuse to let this pain be the loudest voice in my life." It is saying, "I am more than what I have lost. I am more than what they did to me. I am more than what I used to believe about myself."

Letting go means releasing the false narratives that have wrapped themselves around your worth. It means telling the truth that you were hurt, that it mattered, that it changed you but refusing to let that pain define your future. Psalm 34:18 says, "The Lord is close to the broken-hearted and saves those who are crushed in spirit." He does not draw near to our performance. He draws near to our honesty. He comes close when we admit our needs. When we say, "These hurts. I am scared. But I trust You."

Letting go is not a one-time act. Sometimes it happens in layers. Sometimes it feels like you have surrendered it all, only to find yourself clinging to it again the next day. That does not mean you are failing. That means you are human.

It means your healing is alive. It is unfolding. And every time you lay it down again, even if it is the hundredth time, you are practicing freedom. You are loosening its grip on your life. You are choosing to hope over fear, to love over anger, and peace over control.

Forgiveness is one of the hardest forms of letting go. Especially when the wound runs deep and the person who caused it never said they were sorry. Forgiveness does not mean what happened was okay. It does not mean the pain did not matter. It means you are done carrying the poison of bitterness. It means you are choosing to be free. Ephesians 4:31–32 says, "Get rid of all bitterness, rage and anger... forgiving each other, just as in Christ God forgave you." Forgiveness is not saying they were right. It is saying you deserve peace.

Letting go also means surrendering control. For many of us, control was our only sense of stability in a chaotic world. We believed that if we just tried hard enough, stayed vigilant enough, planned enough, we could avoid getting hurt again. But control is an illusion. It is a heavy chain disguised as safety. And the longer we cling to it, the more it exhausts us. Proverbs 3:5 reminds us, "Trust in the Lord with all your heart and lean not on your own understanding." That verse is a lifeline for the one seeking control. It is not a call to blind faith, but to intimate trust in a God who sees the whole picture when we only see pieces.

There will be days when the pain returns. Days when you feel like you have taken steps backward. Days when fear tells you freedom is not for people like you. Do not believe it. You are not starting over. You are still healing. You are still becoming. Letting go is not the end. It is the beginning of becoming. It is the holy space where the Spirit of

God breathes into what was broken and says, "Live." And live, you shall.

The Surrendered Heart

Surrender is not just a concept for the spiritually mature or the emotionally stable. It is not reserved for those who have already found peace or clarity. Surrender is for the broken, the confused, the exhausted, and the barely-hanging-on. It is not about giving up. It is about giving over. It is the sacred act of saying, "I can't carry this anymore, but I believe You can." It is the laying down of our own strength in exchange for God's strength. Not because we are weak, but because we are wise enough to recognize our limits and brave enough to admit our needs.

So many of us were taught to fight through everything.

To hustle our way out of the hurt. To perform strength even when our hearts were breaking. We learned how to survive. We learned how to push through. We learned how to wear resilience like armor. But we were never taught how to surrender. We were never taught that there is a kind of strength found only in release. That there is a sacred beauty in falling into the arms of a God who already knows how tired we are.

The world tells us to keep going. To hustle. To prove ourselves. But Jesus whispers something altogether different. He says, "Come to me. I will give you rest." Not rest after you have earned it. Not rest after you have fixed everything. Rest now. Rest in the middle. Rest while the questions are still unanswered. That is the kind of love that changes everything. A love that meets you where you are, not where you think you should be.

Surrender is not a one-time moment. It is a lifestyle. It is a return. A remembering. A revisiting of trust every single day. Some mornings you will wake up and feel brave.

Other mornings you will wake up with a knot in your stomach and a thousand fears on your chest. Surrender does not mean those moments will not come. It means that when they do, you know where to bring them. It means you know who to trust with the weight you are carrying.

Surrender is not polished. It is not perfect. It is raw. It is holy. It often shows up in the form of tears that fall without permission. In prayers that do not have words. In whispers that barely make it past your lips. It comes when you let go of the need to be impressive and finally allow yourself to be known. Fully seen. Fully loved. Not for your strength, but in your vulnerability.

Healing meets us in that place. Not in our accomplishments. Not in our performance. But in our presence. In our willingness to show up with our brokenness and our belief that God can still do something beautiful with it. It is not about feeling brave. It is about trusting the One who is holding you when you do not.

When you surrender, something shifts. The pressure lifts. The striving stops. And in its place comes peace. Real peace. The kind that does not depend on circumstances.

The kind that flows from the heart of God into the depths of your soul. Surrender makes room for joy to bloom again.

For hope to rise. For beauty to grow in the barren places of your story.

When you finally let go of what was never yours to carry, you begin to see how tightly God was holding you all along. You begin to recognize His voice not in your busyness, but in the stillness. Not in your performance, but in your presence. You begin to feel the tender strength of a Father who never once let you go.

You do not need to know how it all ends. You do not need to see the full map to take the next step. You only need to say yes. Yes, to surrender. Yes, to grace. Yes, to healing. Yes, to becoming. Because what waits on the other side of surrender is not defeat. It is redemption. It is renewal. It is resurrection.

This is not the end of your story. This is the beginning of your becoming.

The Sacred Space of Exhale

Take a moment and breathe. Breathe deep, all the way down into the places that still hold tension. Let your shoulders fall, your jaw soften, your heart settle. Let this truth wrap around you gently, your healing is not behind you. It is happening now. It is not a chapter that has closed. It is a story still being written, one breath at a time.

With every exhale, something is loosening. Every time you choose hope over fear, every time you lay down what was never yours to carry, every time you whisper "help" instead of pretending to be strong, something new is being born. Something holy. Something whole.

You are no longer defined by what broke you. You are not the same woman who once felt like she would never feel joy again. You are no longer carrying shame like it is your name. You are walking lighter. You are standing taller. You are seeing beauty in places where you only seen the debris that the pain left. That is not coincidence. That is healing.

You are learning to live light. You are learning to live loved. You are learning to live led by grace, by peace, by the gentle hand of a God who has never stopped pursuing you.

So, breathe. Exhale. Let the past fall behind you. Let the pressure lift off your shoulders. Let peace fill the places where fear used to reside. Jesus said, "Peace I leave with you. My peace I give you." Not the kind the world offers, but a peace that holds steady in every storm.

There is beauty in your becoming. There is glory in your healing. And there is power in your surrender. You do not have to go back. You do not have to carry it all. You do not have to prove a single thing. You only need to keep breathing. Keep trusting. Keep rising.

Because the soul that exhales, finally and fully, is the soul that is ready to live.

CHAPTER 9

REBUILDING THE
WOMAN WITHIN

The Empty Space Healing Leaves Behind

Healing is often described as a beautiful, redemptive process, and in many ways, that is true. But what is rarely spoken about is what comes after the breakthrough. We do not often talk about the quiet ache that lingers after the crying has stopped, after the release has happened, and after the weight you carried for so long is no longer pressing against your chest. You expect to feel light. You expect to feel whole. And in some ways, you do. But there is also a space that opens, wide and unfamiliar, and it can feel just as heavy as the pain that once filled it.

When you have lived for years with a wound, it becomes part of how you see yourself. Not because you want to, but because pain, over time, can start to feel like home.

You learn how to live with it, how to navigate around it, how to function despite it. You build routines and habits around your survival. You measure days by how heavy your heart feels or how deeply the ache runs. You become so accustomed to the fight that when the war begins to end, your body does not know what to do with the silence. Your soul does not know how to rest in the stillness.

And then God begins to do what only He can. He begins to lift the weight. He begins to unravel the lies you believed about yourself. He begins to soothe the places in you that have never known peace. He begins to whisper into the shadows, bringing healing, not just to the obvious pain, but to the quiet, hidden parts of your soul. And while that healing is good and sacred, it can also feel like exposure. You are lighter, but you are raw. You are free, but you are vulnerable. You are no longer surviving, but you have not quite figured out how to start living either.

There is a strange in-between that comes when the pain leaves but nothing new has settled in yet. A quiet pause. A breath between pages. You look around your life and feel like something is missing, and it is. The pain that used to anchor you, even if it was unhealthy, is gone. And now you are left to discover what will take its place. You are left to learn what it means to live without a limp, what it means to walk without dragging your past behind you. It is unfamiliar, and that unfamiliarity can feel like loss.

But it is not a loss. It is preparation.

The space you feel is not emptiness. It is sacred clearing. God has made room. He has swept away what was never meant to stay so that He can build something better.

You are not empty. You are being prepared for rebuilding.

And that rebuilding begins with rest. It begins with permission to feel everything the confusion, the gratitude, the fear, the wonder. You do not need to rush to fill the space.

You do not need to panic because you do not yet know who you are without your pain. God is not asking you to be finished. He is asking you to be present.

This holy pause, this quiet moment between what was and what is yet to be, is not punishment. It is grace. It is space to breathe. It is space to relearn how to live from a healed place rather than a hurting one. It is the space where your identity begins to rise. It is the space where new dreams are planted, where joy takes root, and where peace begins to grow. This space is not a void. It is the beginning.

So, if you find yourself asking, "Who am I now that I am not carrying all that pain?" you are not lost. You are awakening. You are uncovering the you that has always been there beneath the rubble. You are standing on the threshold of your becoming, and there is no rush. There is only this moment. This breath. This whisper of God reminding you that you are safe, you are seen, and you are exactly where you are supposed to be.

Let yourself settle into the stillness. Let the healing finish its work. Let the quiet be holy. Because this is not the absence of something. It is the presence of something new.

The False Identities We Wore to Survive

Long before we had the words to describe our pain, we developed strategies to live through it. We learned to adapt, to adjust, to fit into molds that made other people comfortable. Without even realizing it, we began to wear our pain like a second skin. It was not a conscious choice.

It was something that happened slowly, over time, because of what we endured. We were not taught how to process our wounds. We were taught how to function despite them. So, we learned to carry what no one could see, and we got good at pretending everything was fine when our hearts were breaking in silence.

Some of us became strong ones. The dependable ones.

The ones who never asked for help and always seemed to hold it together, even when we were crumbling behind closed doors. We convinced ourselves that vulnerability was weakness and strength meant silence. Others of us became peacemakers. We tiptoed around conflict. We kept our voices small. We sacrificed our needs to keep peace, even when that peace cost us our authenticity.

Some of us became achievers, pouring our energy into perfection and productivity because it gave us a sense of value, even if that value was only conditional. And some of us became invisible. We shrank ourselves to fit, to survive, to avoid judgment. We believed being overlooked was safer than being seen and misunderstood.

These roles were never rooted in truth. They were responses to pain. They were shaped by fear, by trauma, by rejection, by abandonment. We wore them like armor because, at the time, they helped us feel safe. We did not know who we were without them, and to be honest, we were too afraid to find out. These false identities became familiar. But familiarity is not the same as freedom. And eventually, the things that once protected us start to confine us.

What once helped you survive is now keeping you stuck.

You may have worn the title of "the reliable one" so long that you forgot how to ask for help. You may have worn the mask of "I'm fine" for so many years that it feels unnatural to say, "I'm not okay." You may have played the role of the fixer in every relationship, believing your worth was tied to what you could do for others. But friend, those roles were not designed for your freedom. They were born out of wounds, and they are no longer serving your healing.

They are not who you are. And they never were.

You were never meant to be defined by what you went through. You were never meant to live your life trying to earn love, affection, or belonging by becoming someone else. You were created in the image of God, intricately designed with intention, identity, and purpose. The fullness of who you are was never supposed to be buried beneath other people's expectations, trauma responses, or survival tactics. You were meant to be known, not managed. You were meant to be free, not confined by the labels the world gave you or the ones you gave yourself out of necessity.

So, this is your invitation to take them off.

Take off the mask of perfection that leaves you exhausted. Lay down the identity of being "the strong one" if it means you never allow yourself to fall apart. Release the need to perform for acceptance or to prove your value. Let go of the idea that being low-maintenance or selfless to a fault is what makes you lovable. It is not. You are lovable simply because you exist. Simply because you are God's.

You are allowed to unlearn the ways you abandoned yourself. You are allowed to stop shrinking to make others comfortable. You are allowed to stop hiding behind busyness, behind humor, behind achievements, behind silence.

You do not have to be everything for everyone. You just must be you. The real you. The one God designed before the world ever tried to tell you who to be.

And if that feels scary, let it. Let it feel unfamiliar. Let it feel tender. That is what healing feels like. That is what reclaiming your identity requires. Not striving more. Not pretending more. But softness. Openness. Honesty.

Honor the version of you who got you here. She fought hard. She endured more than she should have had to. She was brave in ways most people will never know. But now, it is time to become the version of you who can thrive, not just survive. You are not too late. You are not too broken.

You are not beyond the reach of healing. You are becoming. Slowly. Deeply. Beautifully. Becoming.

The old you helped you survive. The real you is going to help you live.

Reclaiming the Truth of Who You Are

There is a moment in every healing journey when you begin to hear the whisper of truth rising above the noise of your past. It does not always come in a loud, dramatic revelation.

Sometimes it comes softly, through a scripture you have read a hundred times but suddenly feel in your bones.

Sometimes it comes through tears that fall when someone looks you in the eye and tells you, "You matter." And sometimes it comes in the stillness, when you begin to wonder if maybe, just maybe, you were never broken beyond repair. That moment is sacred. It is the beginning of reclaiming the truth of who you are.

When pain has been your constant companion, it has a way of distorting your reflection. The trauma, the abandonment, the rejection, the silence—all of it speaks louder than truth if you live with it long enough. You start to believe that you are what happened to you. That you are the mistake you made. That you are the relationship that failed.

That you are the label someone else put on you out of their own brokenness. The enemy of your soul is relentless in trying to convince you that you are damaged goods. That you are too much, or not enough, or somehow at the same time. And after years of hearing those lies, they start to feel like facts.

But here is the truth: you are not your wounds. You are not your worst moments. You are not your silence, your shame, or your scars. You are who God says you are. And He has never changed His mind about you.

He says you are chosen. He says you are set apart. He says you are seen. He says you are valuable, not because of what you do, but because of who you belong to. He calls you His. He delights in you. Not the polished, performative version of you, but the real you. The one with tears in her eyes. The one who questions her worth. The one who feels too tired to keep going. That is the one He loves. That is the one He died for. That is the one He is rebuilding.

Reclaiming your identity is not about earning something new. It is about returning to what was always true before the world tried to tell you otherwise. It is about remembering that your value was established before your story ever began. Before the heartbreak. Before the labels.

Before the fear. God already saw you. Already named you.

Already called you His own.

It is not easy to untangle yourself from the lies you have lived with. It takes time to silence the internal critic that echoes the words of those who hurt you. It takes time to believe that you can be loved without conditions. But healing begins when you stop agreeing with the voice of shame and start aligning your heart with the voice of truth.

The truth that says you are already enough. The truth that says you are already held. The truth that says God has never forgotten who He created you to be.

Sometimes the most courageous thing you can do is look in the mirror and see yourself through God's eyes. Not through the lens of what was done to you. Not through the lens of what you lack. But through the lens of grace.

Through the lens of redemption. Through the lens of love that does not change based on performance. That is the lens that heals. That is the lens that restores.

When you begin to reclaim your identity, you begin to live differently. You speak to yourself with kindness. You set boundaries that protect your peace. You let go of what no longer aligns with the woman you are becoming. You start showing up, not as who others need you to be, but as who God made you to be. Whole. Loved. Seen. And free.

The woman you are becoming is not a stranger to God.

She is not some future version of you that you have to chase down or strive to earn. She is already within you.

God has been nurturing her through every battle, through every surrender, through every hard choice to keep moving forward. She is not perfect. She is not polished. But she is rooted. She is rising. She is real.

You do not have to wait until you feel worthy to believe that you are. You do not have to wait until you understand everything to begin living like you matter. Start where you are. Believe what is true, even if your heart still wavers. God will meet you in that in-between place. He will remind you, again and again, that you are His. That you are enough.

That you are becoming.

Reclaiming the truth of who you are is not a one-time decision. It is a daily return. A constant realignment. A sacred choice to remember. And every time you choose truth over lies, grace over shame, love over fear you are rebuilding. You are becoming.

Learning to See Yourself Through a New Lens

For most of your life, you may have looked at yourself through a lens shaped by pain. A lens fogged with rejection, colored by failure, scratched by disappointment, and warped by shame. That lens does not tell the truth. But when it is the only one you have known, it begins to feel like reality.

You start to believe that your worth is based on what others think of you. You begin to judge yourself by impossible standards, by the wounds you carry, or by the mistakes you made when you were just trying to survive. That old lens distorts who you are, blinding you to the beauty God sees in you every single day.

Learning to see yourself differently is not easy. It requires unlearning the lies. It requires choosing truth when it feels unnatural. It requires holding space for the discomfort that comes when you are no longer defined by what hurt you, but by who created you. At first, it may feel like wearing a pair of glasses that are too strong or not quite the right fit. You feel off balance.

You second guess what you see. You may resist it altogether. But slowly, gently, the view begins to sharpen.

Slowly, your heart begins to open to the possibility that you were never as broken as you once believed. Slowly, you begin to see the reflection God sees when He looks at you—beloved, chosen, radiant, and whole.

Maybe someone complimented you and your first instinct was to reject it. Maybe someone called you brave, and you wanted to laugh or cry because you did not feel brave at all. Maybe someone said you were kind, generous, or worthy, and all you could think was, "If they really knew me, they wouldn't say that." But what if they did? What if they saw the real you?

What if God sees you in the fullness of your becoming, not despite your flaws, but considering your fight? He sees your heart, not just your history. He sees your effort, not just your mistakes. He sees your tenderness, your grit, your longing, your resilience. He sees the woman behind the fear and the faith that brought her here.

You have spent enough of your life being your own harshest critic. You have spent enough time internalizing the voices that told you to stay small, to be quiet, to not take up too much space. But that is not the voice of God.

The voice of God is gentle, not condemning. It is affirming, not shaming. He does not rush you. He does not belittle you. He reminds you. He invites you to see yourself the way He does with compassion, with grace, with honor.

It is time to speak to yourself with the same kindness you pour out to others. It is time to rewrite the script that plays in your mind every time you make a mistake or fall short. You are not unworthy. You are human. And more than that, you are holy, set apart, loved, and known. You do not need to be perfect to be beautiful. You do not need to have it all figured out to be valuable. You are allowed to be both healing and whole, both learning and growing. The goal is not perfection. The goal is truth. And truth says you are enough, even in process.

One of the most powerful shifts you can make in your healing journey is learning to affirm your own worth. Not in arrogance. Not in pride. But in agreement with your Creator. Begin to speak life over yourself. Begin to declare truth, even when it feels foreign. Say it anyway. "I am loved." "I am worthy." "I am growing." "I am not who I was." At first, it may feel strange or forced, but over time, the words will settle into your spirit. And one day, you will believe them not because someone else said so, but because you have finally seen yourself through God's eyes.

Look in the mirror and recognize the woman who did not give up. The one still in the arena. The one who kept walking when it would have been easier to stop. The one who showed up again and again, even when it was hard.

That woman is strong. That woman is becoming. That woman is you. You deserve to be spoken to with love. You deserve to be treated with dignity. You deserve to be seen, not just by others, but by yourself.

Every time you choose grace over criticism, you are shifting the lens. Every time you silence shame and listen to truth, you are changing how you see. And the more you see yourself through the lens of love, the more you will live like a woman who believes she is loved. That is the transformation God desires. Not just for your heart to be healed, but for your eyes to be opened to who you are, to what you carry, and to who you are becoming.

You do not have to wait for others to validate you. You do not have to perform to be enough. You already are. Let that truth become your lens. Let it shape how you think, how you speak to yourself, and how you walk through the world. You are no longer seeing yourself through the eyes of your past. You are seeing yourself through the eyes of grace. And that changes everything.

Small Steps Toward Confidence and Wholeness

Healing is not a straight line. It does not happen all at once.

And it is almost never loud or obvious. Often, healing looks like small, quiet decisions you make when no one else is watching. It is found in the way you speak to yourself in the mirror. It is found in the moments when you choose to rest instead of rushing. It is found in the breath you take before responding to an old trigger, and in the new boundary you set even when your voice trembles. These are the small, sacred steps that carry you closer to wholeness.

There is no finish line to becoming whole. There is no perfect version of what you expect in the future. Wholeness is not about arriving. It is about being present on the journey. It is about choosing truth over fear, grace over guilt, and peace over pressure. It is about waking up each morning and deciding, again and again, to show up for your life. Even when you feel unsure. Even when you still carry questions. Even when the healing is messy and slow. You do not have to have it all figured out. You just have to keep going.

Confidence does not come from perfection. It comes from presence. It grows each time you honor who you are instead of who you think you should be. It grows when you speak up in the room where you used to shrink. It grows when you wear the outfit that makes you feel like yourself again. It grows when you take the risk, try the new thing, or say no when you used to say yes just to be liked. Confidence does not demand attention. It does not shout. It is the quiet knowing that your worth is not up for debate.

Start small. Let confidence build brick by brick. It might look like getting out of bed and making your favorite cup of coffee. It might look like journaling your thoughts when you feel overwhelmed. It might look like speaking kindly to yourself in the middle of a setback. It might look like asking for help when everything in you wants to do it alone. These moments matter. They are not insignificant. They are the foundation of something strong and lasting.

Each small decision to show up with authenticity is a declaration of who you are becoming. Every time you align your actions with the truth of who God says you are, you are reinforcing your identity. When you choose honesty over hiding, presence over performance, and truth over pretending, you are not only healing you are becoming rooted. Grounded. Secure.

The world often teaches us that confidence looks like boldness, achievement, or charisma. But in the Kingdom of

God, confidence is built on trust. Trust in who He is. Trust in who He made you to be. It is not about knowing every-thing. It is about knowing that even in uncertainty, you are held. You are equipped. You are becoming.

Wholeness is not a destination either. It is a practice. It is a posture of honesty. It allows yourself to be both healing and hopeful. Both in process and in purpose. Wholeness means no longer trying to return to who you were before the pain. It means letting God shape you into someone new, someone stronger, softer, wiser, and more anchored in grace. It is not about being untouched by life. It is about being transformed by it.

You will start to feel the shift, not always in big, lifechanging ways, but in the subtle patterns that begin to break. You will notice it in the way you pause before falling back into old habits. In the way you respond with compassion instead of criticism. In the way you rest without guilt.

In the way you start to believe that your needs matter. That your voice matters. That your story is sacred and worth honoring.

These shifts are holy. They are evidence that healing is working. That you are being rebuilt from the inside out.

That you are learning to live in alignment with your true self, not the version you were forced to become in survival. You are healing at a soul level. You are allowing God to restore what life tried to steal. You are becoming whole, not because you fixed yourself, but because you allowed Him to guide the process.

Let the work be slow. Let it be messy. Let it be tender.

You do not have to rush what is holy. There is no shame in taking your time. Each step, no matter how small, is sacred.

Each moment of awareness, each breath of surrender, each act of self-kindness is evidence of your courage.

You are not just rebuilding a life. You are building a legacy. One rooted in grace, marked by faith, and sustained by love. And every single small step you take matters more than you know.

You're Already Becoming Her

It might not look like you imagined. The healing. The transformation. The becoming. Maybe it feels slower than you hoped. Maybe it has been more painful than you expected.

Maybe you still wake up some days wondering if any of it is even working. Maybe when you look in the mirror, all you see is someone trying her best to hold it together. Someone who still doubts. Still wrestles. Still aches. But let me gently remind you of a truth that runs deeper than how you feel right now.

You are already becoming her.

Not the perfect version of you. Not the version without pain or questions or scars. But the healed version. The whole version. The grounded, grace-soaked version of you that God saw from the very beginning. She is not waiting for you in some distant, unreachable future. She is being formed in every quiet moment you choose to stay, to try, to pray, to surrender. She is the woman who kept walking when everything in her wanted to give up. She is in the tears you cried when no one else saw. She is in the boundaries you set, in the no you finally voiced, in the gentle yes to start again.

You are already becoming her in the pause before you react, in the peace you protect, in the honest way you speak to your heart. She is in the brave things you have done that no one else applauded. She is in the healing you have carried forward even when no one else understood the weight of what you were breaking free from. Becoming is not a moment. It is a rhythm. A process. A becoming that unfolds with grace, not performance.

She is the woman who knows her worth without needing to prove it. The one who has stopped chasing perfection and started embracing her humanity. The one who no longer needs to be chosen by others to know she is already chosen by God. She is the woman who walks with quiet strength, who does not need to shout to be heard because her presence carries peace. She sets boundaries with love, honors her emotions, protects her joy, and invites others into her life with discernment and care. She does not hide.

She does not shrink. She rises.

She is the woman who forgives herself for the years she spent trying to be what others expected. The woman who no longer let's fear write the next chapter. The woman who walks forward, not because the road is easy, but because she finally believes she is worth the journey. She laughs again not because everything is perfect, but because she has tasted joy in the middle of sorrow. She believes again not because she has all the answers, but because she has seen God's faithfulness even in the unanswered prayers.

You do not have to hustle to become her. You do not have to earn her with effort. You only need to keep showing up. Keep surrendering. Keep choosing the truth. Keep giving God access to the places in you that still feel tender. He is not asking you to finish. He is asking you to be faithful.

To believe that this work He is doing in you is real, even when it is quiet. To trust that your slow becoming is no less holy than someone else's loud transformation.

This is not the end of your healing. It is the unfolding of your wholeness. The beginning of your deeper becoming. It is what happens when you stop striving and start receiving. When you stop hiding and start living. When you stop defining yourself by your pain and start embracing your purpose. This is the start of something sacred. Something lasting. Something true.

You are not behind. You are not broken. You are not failing. You are already becoming her.

Let that truth settle into your bones. Let it soften the parts of you that are still uncertain. Let it speak to the version of you who wonders if it is too late. Because it is not.

You are still here. You are still becoming.

CHAPTER 10

WHEN HEALING BECOMES HOME

The Quiet After Survival

There is a moment in healing that no one prepares you for.

It does not arrive with celebration or certainty. It does not announce itself with relief loud enough to convince you that the worst is behind you. Instead, it comes quietly, of-ten after the hardest work has already been done. It is the moment when survival is no longer necessary, but you are not yet sure how to live without it.

For a long time, healing required effort. It demanded courage, honesty, and the willingness to stay present with what hurt instead of escaping it. It meant naming wounds you had learned to ignore and facing truths that once felt too heavy to carry. It required revisiting memories that had shaped you and allowing yourself to feel what you once numbed. Healing was not passive. It was intentional, exhausting, and deeply brave.

And then something unexpected happened.

The pain loosened its grip.

Not in a dramatic way. Not all at once. But enough that the constant urgency began to soften. Enough that you no longer woke up braced for impact. Enough that your body started to settle, even if your mind had not caught up yet.

You could breathe without guarding your chest. You could sit in silence without panic rising. And instead of feeling relief, you felt unfamiliar.

There is a disorientation that comes when healing settles in. The chaos that once filled every corner of your life begins to recede, and suddenly there is space. Space where fear once lived. Space where pain once dictated your responses. Space where survival once ruled every decision.

And in that open space, a quiet question begins to rise.

Who am I now?

That question can feel unsettling because it asks you to live differently. It asks you to imagine a life not governed by fear or endurance. It asks you to trust that safety can exist without constant vigilance. And that kind of trust does not come easily to those who have learned to survive by staying alert.

When Survival Is No Longer the Identity

I did not realize how deeply survival had shaped my identity until I no longer needed it. Pain had become a reference point for how I moved through the world. It influenced how guarded I remained in relationships, how quickly I anticipated disappointment, and how often I dismissed my own needs. Even healing itself became something I worked toward, something I focused on daily, something that quietly defined me.

Survival had taught me how to endure, but it had not taught me how to live.

When the urgency eased, I found myself standing in unfamiliar territory. I was no longer fighting to stay afloat, yet I did not know how to rest. I was no longer hiding, yet

being fully seen still felt risky. I was no longer the woman I had been in survival, but I was not yet confident in the woman I was becoming.

This was not failure. This was not regression. This was transition.

Healing does not stop at relief. It moves toward integration. Toward learning how to live from wholeness rather than constantly tending to wounds. But that shift can feel unsettling, especially when pain has been your companion for most of your life.

Survival mode has structure. It gives you rules. It tells you when to speak, when to stay quiet, when to brace yourself. Wholeness, on the other hand, asks you to trust. It invites you to rest. It challenges you to believe that safety is not temporary.

Learning to live healed requires a different kind of courage. Not the courage to endure pain, but the courage to believe you no longer have to.

Letting Go of the Roles That Once Protected You

There are identities we wear to stay alive. The strong one.

The agreeable one. The dependable one. The one who never needs help. These roles once served a purpose. They protected you when you had no other choice. They helped you navigate environments where vulnerability was not safe.

But healing invites you to loosen your grip on them.

Not because they were wrong, but because they are no longer required.

For a long time, my worth was measured by how well I held everything together. I believed that being low maintenance made me lovable. I believed that silence equaled maturity. I believed that strength meant never needing anything. These beliefs did not vanish overnight. They were reinforced over years and embedded deeply within me.

So, when healing created space, my instinct was to fill it. To stay busy. To remain useful. To find something else to fix. Stillness felt dangerous. Peace felt unfamiliar. Joy felt undeserved.

But God does not heal us so we can remain braced for impact. He heals us so we can rest without fear.

Letting go of survival roles does not mean forgetting what you endured. It means acknowledging that those versions of you did their job and honoring them without allowing them to define your future.

Learning What Home Actually Feels Like

Home does not mean perfect. Home does not mean untouched by pain. Home means safe enough to exhale.

Healing became home for me when I stopped questioning whether I deserved the quiet. When I stopped waiting for everything to fall apart again. When I allowed myself to believe that stability was not a temporary pause, but something I was allowed to build my life upon.

This shift did not happen suddenly. It unfolded slowly, through small but meaningful changes that were easy to overlook if I was not paying attention.

I noticed I was no longer scanning rooms for danger. I noticed I could speak honestly without rehearsing. I noticed I could rest without guilt following me. I noticed I trusted my voice instead of silencing it.

Each moment felt ordinary on its own, but together they changed how I lived. Healing was no longer something I worked toward. It became something I lived from.

Living From Wholeness Instead of Fear

The truth is simple, but learning to live it takes time.

You are not who you were in survival. But you are also not required to rush into a new version of yourself.

There is a holy middle ground where identity settles gently. Where you are no longer defined by what hurt you, but you are also not pressured to prove how far you have come. This is the space where healing moves from something you *do* into something you *live from*. And for many, this space feels unfamiliar, even uncomfortable, because it does not operate on urgency or fear.

Fear has a way of disguising itself as wisdom. It tells you to stay guarded. To stay alert. To stay ready. It convinces you that peace is fragile and joy should be held loosely because it could disappear at any moment. Living from wholeness asks you to challenge that narrative. It invites you to believe that peace does not have to be earned or defended constantly.

This is where God does some of His quietest work.

He does not demand that you rush into confidence. He does not pressure you to perform healing. He does not scold you for lingering hesitation. Instead, He invites you to abide. To remain. To trust that you are held even when you are not striving.

Abiding requires a surrender that feels vulnerable. It asks you to sit with yourself without judgment. To notice old reactions without condemning yourself for them. To respond to fear with compassion rather than shame. I had to learn that noticing an old pattern did not mean healing had failed. It meant healing was deep enough for awareness to exist.

Healing is not undone by discomfort. Growth is not erased by doubt. Wholeness is not fragile.

It is resilient. It bends without breaking. It allows space for humanity without collapsing under it.

Living from wholeness means learning how to pause instead of react. It means choosing curiosity over criticism when something feels off. It means allowing yourself to be human without interpreting it as weakness. Fear may still whisper, but it no longer gets the final word.

When Peace Becomes Ordinary

One of the most surprising parts of healing is how quietly peace arrives. It does not always feel euphoric or dramatic.

Sometimes it feels almost underwhelming, especially if your nervous system has been conditioned to chaos. When peace first entered my life consistently, I did not recognize it right away. It felt unfamiliar. Suspicious. Too calm.

I had learned to equate intensity with meaning. If something felt steady, I assumed it would not last. If a season felt gentle, I waited for disruption. Healing required me to relearn what safety felt like in my body, not just in my mind.

Peace became ordinary in subtle ways.

I paused before reacting. I listened to my body instead of overriding it. I trusted my instincts without second guessing myself. I rested without needing to justify it.

These shifts were quiet, but they mattered. I was no longer governed by urgency. I was guided by discernment. And discernment grew from knowing myself, trusting myself, and believing that God was not leading me into peace only to snatch it away.

When peace becomes ordinary, joy no longer needs permission. Rest no longer feels indulgent. You stop apologizing for your softness. You stop explaining your boundaries. You stop questioning whether calm means complacency. You learn that peace is not a lack of passion. It is the presence of alignment.

Healing becomes home when peace no longer feels like something you must protect at all costs. It becomes something you trust. Something you build from. Something that anchors you when life still brings challenges, because it will.

Peace does not mean life stops being hard. It means you stop living braced for collapse.

Grieving What Was Lost Without Living There

There is grief that accompanies healing, and it deserves to be named. Not grief that pulls you backward, but grief that honors what was lost along the way. Grief for the woman who never felt safe enough to rest. Grief for the years spent surviving instead of living. Grief for the tenderness that was interrupted too soon.

I had to allow myself to grieve without guilt. To acknowledge the cost of what I endured without minimizing it or rushing toward gratitude. Healing does not require you to be grateful for what hurt you. It allows you to be honest about what it took from you.

Grief does not negate healing. It completes it.

When you honor what was lost, you give dignity to your story. You allow yourself to feel compassion for who you were without becoming trapped in who you had to be. God does not rush this part. He knows that grief held with grace does not destroy. It deepens.

There were days when I wanted certainty. When I wanted a clear label for who I was now. But God did not offer me a title. He offered me presence. And presence was enough.

Grieving without living there means allowing the ache to exist without letting it define you. It means carrying the past with gentleness rather than letting it lead you. It means trusting that honoring what was lost does not threaten what is being built.

Standing on the Threshold of Becoming

Learning to live healed means learning to live unarmored. It means letting yourself feel without bracing. Trusting connection without overanalyzing. Choosing rest without apology. Believing that peace does not have to be earned.

This is not the end of the journey. It is the foundation.

From here, something stronger can rise. Something embodied. Something confident. Something rooted in truth rather than fear. Becoming Her is not about striving for a future version of yourself. It is about allowing what has been healed to shape how you live now.

This chapter stands at the threshold.

Not between broken and healed, but between healing and embodiment. Between knowing and living. Between tending wounds and walking in wholeness.

You do not have to rush forward. You do not have to prove readiness. You are allowed to stand here, grounded and present, trusting that who you are becoming is already unfolding.

Becoming Her begins quietly. It begins when healing feels like home. When peace feels trustworthy. When identity feels anchored.

When you stop chasing who you think you should be and begin honoring who you already are. And that is sacred ground.

CHAPTER 11

STANDING IN HER STRENGTH

When Healing Begins to Take Shape

There comes a moment in the healing journey when something shifts beneath the surface, and it is so subtle that you almost miss it. There is no announcement. No clear line drawn in the sand between before and after. Yet once it happens, you cannot return to who you were. Something has settled. Something has rooted. Something has changed.

For a long time, healing felt like effort. Like constant attention. Like tending wounds that reopened easily if left

unattended. You learned how to scan your inner world for pain, how to trace reactions back to their source, how to stay present when your instinct was to flee. You did the work slowly, imperfectly, often without reassurance that it was making a difference.

And then one day, you realize you are no longer scrambling.

You are standing.

Not because everything is resolved, but because the ground beneath you no longer shifts with every emotion or memory. The urgency that once drove you has softened.

The fear that once dictated your choices has loosened its grip. You still feel deeply, but you are no longer consumed by what you feel.

This is the moment when healing stops being something you actively manage and starts becoming something you live from.

You are no longer gathering pieces of yourself from the wreckage. You are no longer asking whether you will ever feel whole. You are beginning to inhabit the woman you fought so hard to reclaim.

Pause here. Let that land.

You did not bypass this season. You did not rush toward relief. You stayed present through discomfort. You faced truths that were painful to admit. You allowed yourself to grieve, to rage, to soften, to question, and to hope again. That is not small work. That is courageous, life altering work.

The steadiness you feel now did not come easily. It was earned through honesty and endurance, through choosing healing again and again when it would have been easier to numb or distract. The fact that you are standing now is evidence that something strong has been built beneath you.

Recognizing the Strength That Was Built Quietly

Strength does not always look like power. Sometimes it looks like restraint. Like patience. Like learning how to respond instead of react. Strength often forms quietly, without recognition, and because of that, it is easy to overlook how much has changed.

Think about who you were at the beginning of this journey. Think about how quickly your body moved into fear. How often your mind raced ahead to worst case scenarios. How deeply you questioned yourself. How frequently you dismissed your own needs.

Now notice what is different. You pause where you once panicked. You speak where you once stayed silent.

You rest where you once pushed through exhaustion. You listen to yourself instead of overriding your intuition. These are not small shifts. They are signs of deep internal strength.

I did not recognize my own strength in the moment it was forming. I noticed it later, looking back. I noticed it in how my voice steadied. In how my decisions aligned with peace instead of fear. In how I no longer rehearsed conversations in my head before speaking. In how I trusted myself to handle discomfort without unraveling.

That strength did not arrive overnight.

It was built through consistency.

Every time you honored your limits, strength grew.

Every time you told the truth instead of avoiding it, strength deepened. Every time you stayed present instead of dissociating, strength took root.

Healing did not only soften you. It fortified you.

You are no longer standing on unstable ground, wondering whether you will collapse under pressure. You have already endured pressure. You have already survived storms that changed you. What stands beneath you now is not fragile. It is grounded.

No Longer Shrinking to Be Safe

One of the clearest signs that healing has taken hold is the absence of shrinking. Shrinking to avoid conflict.

Shrinking to preserve relationships. Shrinking to stay acceptable. Shrinking to survive.

For a long time, shrinking felt like wisdom. You learned how to read the room, how to anticipate reactions, how to make yourself smaller so others would feel more comfortable. You learned how to disappear just enough to stay safe. But healing slowly dismantles the need for self-erasure.

At some point, you began to feel resistance rise when you tried to shrink again. The old reflex no longer fit. Staying quiet felt heavier than speaking. Abandoning yourself felt more painful than disappointing others. And that was not rebellion. That was growth.

You stopped silencing your needs to avoid discomfort.

You stopped apologizing for boundaries. You stopped contorting yourself to fit expectations that were never yours to carry. And you did not become hard. You became honest.

There is a sacred difference between being soft and being small. Softness is openness. Smallness is self-betrayal.

Standing in strength does not require force or aggression. It requires alignment. It means your inner world and outer world begin to tell the same story.

Your yes carries clarity now. Your no, no longer comes with explanation. Your presence no longer asks for permission.

That is not arrogance. That is embodiment. That is what happens when you stop negotiating your worth and start honoring your truth.

Trusting the Woman, You Are Becoming

There is a sacred trust that forms when you stop doubting your own growth. When you stop searching for evidence that you are healed enough. When you stop waiting for permission to step forward with confidence. Trust is not something you declare. It is something you build through relationship with yourself.

You trust yourself now because you have walked with yourself through the hardest parts. You have seen how you respond under pressure. You have learned how you recover when things feel unsteady. You have watched yourself choose healing even when it was lonely, slow, or misunderstood.

That matters more than you know.

You no longer need constant reassurance. You no longer need to explain your boundaries. You no longer need validation for choices that align with your peace.

You trust the woman you are becoming because she has proven herself.

She stayed when it was hard. She told the truth when it was uncomfortable. She chose growth when it required patience.

That trust does not shout. It steadies. It anchors. It allows you to move forward without second guessing every step.

Strength That Does Not Rush the Future

One of the clearest signs that healing has matured into strength is the absence of urgency. You no longer feel chased by who you should be or pressured by how far you still have to go. You are not scrambling to become something impressive. You are no longer measuring your worth by productivity, performance, or progress.

You are grounded enough to wait.

This kind of strength does not rush the future because it is no longer afraid of the present. It understands that becoming is not something you force, but something you allow. You are no longer living from a place of panic, trying to outrun your past or prove that you are healed enough to move forward.

You trust the process now.

There was a time when uncertainty felt threatening.

When not knowing what is going to come next caused anxiety to rise in your chest. But healing taught you how to stay. How to breathe through the unknown. How to trust that clarity unfolds with time and obedience, not pressure.

This strength knows how to pause without fear. It knows how to move without forcing. It knows how to wait without doubting.

And because of that, it lasts.

You are no longer driven by fear of falling apart. You already know you can withstand discomfort. You have lived through seasons that demanded everything you had, and you are still here. That knowledge settles deeply. It changes how you approach what comes next.

You are not late. You are not behind. You are exactly where growth can continue to unfold.

Celebrating the Distance You Have Traveled

Before you move any closer to what comes next, you need to stop and truly see how far you have come. Not intellectually. Not politely. But honestly.

There was a version of you who did not think healing was possible. A version of you who believed this pain would always define you. A version of you who felt trapped inside patterns you did not choose but could not escape. That version of you still exists in your memory, and she deserves to be honored.

Look at the distance between her and who you are now.

You are more aware. You are more compassionate. You are more anchored. You are more honest.

You no longer abandon yourself the way you once did.

You no longer ignore your needs. You no longer tolerate what costs you your peace simply to keep others comfortable. These shifts may not be visible to the outside world, but they are monumental inside of you.

Growth like this is quiet, but it is profound.

You did not arrive here by accident. You arrived here because you chose to stay present. You chose to keep going. You chose to do the inner work even when it felt lonely or slow. Healing does not reward effort immediately, but it does reward faithfulness.

And you were faithful.

Naming the Wins No One Applauded

There are victories in healing that no one celebrates because no one else can see them. But they are victories nonetheless, and they deserve to be named.

You learned how to sit with discomfort without escaping it. You learned how to speak truth without softening it to be palatable. You learned how to listen to your body instead of dismissing it. You learned how to rest without guilt chasing you afterward.

You stopped betraying yourself in small ways. You stopped explaining your boundaries. You stopped apologizing for needing space, time, or clarity. These changes did not happen overnight. They made one decision at a time.

And they matter.

The world may not applaud these wins, but they are the foundation of everything that comes next. Strength built quietly is strength that cannot be taken from you.

Carrying Confidence Without Performance

As you stand here, something else has shifted too. Confidence has begun to rise, not as bravado or certainty, but as grounded assurance. You no longer need to perform strength to feel secure. You no longer need to prove your worth to take up space.

Confidence now lives in your posture. In your voice. In your willingness to stay true to yourself.

This confidence does not seek attention. It does not compete. It does not need affirmation. It exists because you trust yourself to respond with wisdom and compassion, no matter what unfolds.

That kind of confidence is unshakeable.

It does not mean you will never doubt again. It means doubt no longer defines you. You know how to meet it without collapsing. You know how to stay anchored even when old fears whisper.

You are no longer trying to become strong. You already are.

The Sacred Pause Before Becoming

This chapter is not the finish line. It is the pause before movement. The moment where everything slows just enough for you to recognize the strength that has been formed within you.

You are no longer bracing for impact. You are no longer preparing to survive. You are no longer waiting to feel ready.

You are ready because you are grounded.

This is the moment when breath deepens. When shoulders settle. When the noise quiets enough for clarity to rise. It is the moment before Becoming Her steps fully into the light.

And it matters that you linger here for a moment.

Not to question yourself. Not to doubt what is next. But to honor what has been built.

Because what rises next does not come from striving. It comes from strength already formed.

Standing on the Edge of Who You Are Becoming

You are standing at the edge now. Not between broken and healed, but between healing and embodiment. Between knowing and living. Between preparation and expression.

Everything you have done has led here. From this place, Becoming Her is not an aspiration. It is a continuation. A natural unfolding of the work you have already done.

She does not arrive suddenly. She rises gradually, confidently, and without apology.

You do not have to force her emergence. You do not have to perfect yourself first. You do not have to prove anything. You are strong enough to step forward because you are anchored. And that is enough.

CHAPTER 12

LIVING FROM WHAT WAS HEALED

Becoming Was Never About Arrival

For a long time, becoming felt like something that lived in the future. A version of yourself you would reach once enough healing had happened, once enough time had passed, once enough strength had been gathered. Becoming sounded like arrival. Like certainty. Like a finish line waiting somewhere ahead.

But that was never what becoming truly meant.

Becoming was never about finally getting it right. It was never about erasing the past or outgrowing the woman you once were. It was never about perfection, clarity, or having all the answers neatly arranged.

Becoming was always about integration.

It was about learning how to live honestly inside the life you already have. It was about allowing healing to change how you move through the world, not just how you understand yourself. It was about standing fully present in your own skin, no longer fragmented by survival, fear, or self abandonment.

You did not become her all at once. You became her in moments.

Moments when you stayed instead of numbing. Moments when you told the truth instead of shrinking. Moments when you rested instead of pushing. Moments when you chose alignment over approval.

These moments were not dramatic. They were faithful.

And together, they changed everything.

Becoming Her is not a destination you reach. It is a posture you inhabit. It is how you stand in your life now, aware, grounded, and awake.

The Woman Who Walked Through the Fire

Before you can fully step into who you are becoming, you must honor who carried you here.

There was a woman who walked through fire to arrive at this place. A woman who endured seasons she did not choose and pain she did not deserve. A woman who learned how to survive long before she learned how to feel safe. She adapted. She coped. She carried more than anyone ever knew.

That woman deserves recognition. She did not fail because she struggled. She did not break because she hurt. She did not lose herself because she did what she had to do to survive. She was resourceful. She was resilient. She was strong in ways she never asked to be.

And eventually, she became brave enough to lay survival down.

She chose to feel. She chose to face the truth. She chose to heal even when it was slow.

That choice changed the trajectory of her life.

The woman you are now did not replace her. She integrated her. She took the strength survival built and softened it with compassion. She took the awareness pain taught her and shaped it into wisdom. She took the endurance she learned in the dark and transformed it into grounded confidence.

You are not becoming despite what you survived. You are becoming because of what you learned.

The fire did not consume you. It refined you.

And now, you stand with both strength and tenderness intact.

Living as Her in Ordinary Days

Becoming Her does not require a new life. It requires a new way of inhabiting the one you already have. For a long time, you may have believed that transformation would announce itself through dramatic change.

A new environment.

A new role.

A new season that finally proves you have arrived.

But what you are learning now is quieter and far more powerful. Becoming Her shows up in the ordinary days that once felt insignificant.

It shows up when you wake without dread. When you move through your morning without bracing. When you make decisions from clarity rather than fear.

These are not small shifts. They are the evidence of a life no longer governed by survival.

You live as Her when you listen to yourself without argument. When you trust your instincts instead of outsourcing your authority. When you allow your pace to reflect your peace instead of your pressure. You no longer need life to look different in order to feel different within it.

Her presence is not dependent on circumstances. It is anchored in alignment.

You notice this in how you respond to interruption. In how you handle disappointment. In how you recover when something does not go as planned. There is steadiness now where chaos once lived. There is patience where urgency once ruled. There is grace where self-judgment once dominated.

This is what it means to live embodied. You are no longer watching your life from the outside, waiting for it to begin. You are inside it, engaged, awake, and present.

Strength That Holds Without Hardening

One of the most beautiful outcomes of healing is the kind of strength it produces. Not the brittle strength that comes from forcing your way through pain. Not the hardened strength that keeps everything at a distance. But a strength that can hold weight without closing itself off.

This strength does not flinch at discomfort. It does not collapse under pressure. It does not need to dominate to feel secure.

It is quiet. It is grounded. It is flexible.

You carry this strength now in how you navigate boundaries. You do not build them out of defensiveness. You build them out of clarity. You know where you end and where others begin. You know what you can offer and what you cannot. And you trust yourself to honor that without guilt.

You carry this strength in how you remain open without being exposed. You allow connection, but you do not abandon yourself to maintain it. You care deeply, but you no longer carry what is not yours. This balance once felt impossible. Now it feels natural.

Strength like this was not given to you. It was forged.

It was shaped in moments where you chose honesty over harmony. In moments where you rested instead of proving. In moments where you let yourself be seen without controlling the outcome. Each of those moments strengthened your capacity to remain whole.

You are no longer afraid of your own depth. You are no longer intimidated by your own presence.

You trust yourself to remain intact.

Confidence That Does Not Need Validation

Confidence, in this season, feels different than it once did. It does not announce itself. It does not compete. It does not seek reassurance. It simply exists.

You no longer measure yourself against others to determine your worth. You no longer wait for affirmation to confirm your choices. You no longer need external agreement to stand by what feels true.

This confidence is not rooted in certainty. It is rooted in self-trust. You trust yourself to listen, to adjust and to respond with integrity when things shift. Because of that, you move through the world with a quiet authority that does not demand recognition. You speak when it matters.

You remain silent when it does not. You choose intentionally rather than reactively.

There was a time when you needed validation to feel safe. That need made sense. You were learning how to survive. But now, survival is no longer your operating system.

You are living from alignment, not fear.

Confidence becomes your baseline, not your armor.

You no longer perform strength. You embody it.

Claiming Space Without Apology

As you live more fully as Her, something else changes. You stop apologizing for taking up space.

You stop shrinking your voice to make others comfortable. You stop minimizing your needs to avoid inconvenience. You stop diluting your truth to maintain approval.

This does not make you harsh. It makes you honest.

You claim space by existing fully. By speaking clearly. By honoring your limits. By trusting that you do not need to earn your place. You belong because you are here.

This claiming is not aggressive. It is grounded. It does not push others away. It invites the right connections closer.

You are no longer negotiating your worth. You are living from it.

Walking Forward With Clarity and Grace

There is a noticeable difference between moving forward because you are driven and moving forward because you are clear. Drive pushes. Clarity guides. For much of your life, forward motion may have been fueled by urgency, by the need to escape pain, by the hope that the next season will finally bring relief.

That is not what moves you now. You walk forward with grace because you are no longer running from who you were. You are carrying her with you, integrated and honored. The past no longer pulls at you from behind. It informs you, but it does not define your direction.

Clarity does not mean certainty. It means alignment. It means your steps match your values. It means you move with intention instead of impulse. It means you no longer force outcomes to feel secure.

You trust yourself enough to take the next right step without needing the entire path revealed.

Grace shows up in how you respond when things do not unfold as expected. You do not spiral. You do not self-abandon. You do not interpret challenge as failure. You adjust. You listen. You remain steady.

This grace was earned. It came from learning how to stay present with discomfort without turning against yourself. It came from choosing compassion over criticism. It came from allowing yourself to be human without shame.

You are no longer harsh with yourself when you falter. You are no longer rigid in how you define success.

You move forward with a gentleness that does not weaken you. It strengthens you.

Choosing Your Life With Intention

Becoming Her is not something that happens to you. It is something you choose, again and again, in the small decisions that shape your days.

You choose how you spend your time. You choose what you give your energy to. You choose which voices influence you.

These choices are no longer reactive. They are deliberate. You are aware of what drains you and what sustains you. You recognize when something no longer aligns and you allow yourself to let it go without dramatizing the release.

You no longer live on autopilot. You are awake to your life.

This intentionality does not make your world smaller. It makes it clearer. It creates space for what matters. It allows your life to reflect who you are now, not who you had to be before.

You choose presence over perfection. You choose honesty over harmony. You choose depth over distraction.

These choices may not always be visible to others, but they shape everything you experience.

You are no longer waiting for permission to live fully.

You are choosing it.

Becoming as an Ongoing Unfolding

There is a relief that comes when you realize that becoming is not something you finish. It is something you live.

You are no longer striving to arrive at a final version of yourself. You understand now that growth is not linear and wholeness is not static. You will continue to change, to learn, to refine. And that is not a threat to who you are. It is an expression of life.

Becoming Her does not lock you into an identity. It frees you to continue evolving. You trust that you can grow without losing yourself. You trust that new seasons will not erase the grounding you have built. You trust that expansion does not require you to abandon what has stabilized you.

This trust allows you to remain open. Curious. Engaged.

You do not cling to who you are today out of fear that change will undo you. You welcome growth because you know how to stay rooted while you stretch.

Becoming becomes a rhythm rather than a goal. A way of engaging with life rather than a standard you must meet. You are no longer chasing wholeness. You are living from it.

Carrying Authority Without Dominance

As you step more fully into who you are, you may notice a quiet authority emerging. Not the kind that demands attention or control, but the kind that comes from self-possession.

You know who you are. You know what you value. You know what you will no longer tolerate.

That knowing changes how you show up.

You speak with clarity instead of over explaining. You set boundaries without apology. You make decisions without needing consensus. This authority does not push others down. It invites respect.

You do not need to dominate to feel secure. You do not need to convince others to validate your choices. You stand in your life with confidence because you are no longer fragmented.

Authority like this is calm. It is steady. It is rooted in integrity rather than control. You are not trying to be powerful. You are aligned. And alignment carries its own weight.

The Woman This Journey Was Always Shaping

From the very beginning, this journey was never only about healing pain. It was about reclaiming presence. It was about learning how to stay connected to yourself when life demanded more than you thought you could give. It was about discovering that strength does not disappear when you soften and that wholeness does not require forgetting what you have endured.

Every chapter of this story has been shaping you for this moment.

Not so you could finally be done. But so you could finally be rooted.

You have learned how to name what hurts without letting it define you. You have learned how to face the truth without collapsing beneath it. You have learned how to carry compassion for the woman you were while standing firmly as the woman you are now.

That is not small work. That is becoming.

The wreckage did not have the final word. The pain did not determine the ending. The silence did not swallow you whole. Instead, each moment of honesty, each act of courage, each quiet choice to stay present reshaped you from the inside out.

You are not standing here because everything was easy. You are standing here because you did not turn away.

No Longer Living in Reaction to the Past

One of the most profound shifts in becoming is this. You are no longer living in reaction to what happened. The past may still exist in memory, but it no longer governs your movement. It no longer dictates your pace. It no longer defines your worth.

You are not orienting your life around what broke you.

You are orienting it around what is true.

This changes how you move forward. You no longer make decisions to avoid pain. You make them to honor alignment. You no longer brace yourself for disappointment. You trust yourself to respond when challenges arise.

You no longer shrink to stay safe. You remain present because safety has been rebuilt from within.

The woman you are now does not need to prove that she is healed. She lives from healing as a quiet strength that supports her every step.

Living Awake in a Life That Is Yours

Becoming Her means waking up inside your own life.

It means no longer waiting for permission to take up space.

No longer asking whether you are allowed to want more.

No longer negotiating your worth through effort or endurance.

You live awake when you choose yourself without apology. When you speak with clarity instead of caution. When you allow joy without suspicion and rest without guilt. You are no longer measuring your life by how much you can handle. You are measuring it by how honestly you inhabit it.

This is what it means to live as Her. Not perfect. Not untouched by struggle. But present, grounded, and intentional.

You are not disconnected from your body. You listen when it asks for care. You are not disconnected from your truth. You honor it even when it asks you to change. You are not disconnected from your values. They guide you quietly, steadily, faithfully.

This is not a dramatic transformation. It is a sustainable one.

The Strength You Carry Forward

As this book comes to a close, what you carry forward matters more than what you leave behind. You carry self-trust, discernment, and the ability to pause, listen, and choose.

You carry the knowledge that you can survive discomfort without losing yourself.

You carry the confidence that comes from having faced hard truths and remained standing. You carry the freedom that comes from no longer needing to be someone else to be enough.

The strength you carry now is not loud. It does not dominate. It does not demand recognition. It holds space. It steadies you. It allows you to move forward without fear. This strength will guide you into whatever comes next.

Choosing Her, Again and Again

Becoming Her is not a moment you check off. It is a commitment you renew.

You choose her when you listen instead of override.

You choose her when you rest instead of prove. You choose her when you speak truth instead of staying silent.

These choices will continue to shape your life. Some days will feel clear. Others will feel uncertain. But you no longer fear uncertainty. You trust yourself to navigate it.

You do not need to rush. You do not need to arrive. You do not need to become anything else.

You are already living as the woman this journey has been forming.

The Ending That Is Also a Beginning

This book does not end with answers. It ends with readiness. Readiness to live from truth rather than fear. Readiness to carry wholeness into ordinary days. Readiness to stand grounded, open, and awake.

You are not stepping into something fragile. You are stepping from something solid. The woman you are now is not waiting to be discovered. She is already here, present in your breath, your posture, your choices.

You are not becoming her someday. You are becoming her every day.

And that is how this story continues.

The Ending That Becomes Her Choice

This book does not end with a quiet release or a gentle fade out. It ends with a decision. Not one made in urgency or fear, but one made from grounding, from clarity, from a deep internal knowing that you are no longer waiting to become someone else. You are choosing to live as her.

She is the woman who no longer needs permission. The woman who trusts her voice and honors both her limits and her longings. The woman who no longer abandons herself in order to belong. She is not reckless or hardened. She is rooted. She knows who she is, and she no longer negotiates that truth for comfort or approval.

You are not stepping forward unsure of your footing. You are stepping forward from solid ground. Everything you have faced, everything you have felt, everything you have named and healed has strengthened the foundation beneath you. You are not fragile here. You are formed.

What once threatened to undo you has instead shaped you into someone who can stand with confidence and clarity.

This is not the end of the work. It is the beginning of ownership. Ownership of your life, your presence, and the space you take up in the world. You are no longer shrinking your truth to stay comfortable. You are no longer editing yourself to be acceptable. You are no longer waiting for confidence to arrive before you act. You are acting from confidence that has already been built.

You know how to listen to yourself now. You know how to pause instead of panic. You know how to choose alignment over approval. That knowledge will carry you forward.

It will steady you when life shifts. It will guide you when decisions feel unclear. It will remind you who you are when old patterns try to resurface.

Whatever comes next does not require a different version of you. It requires this one. The woman who learned how to stay when it was uncomfortable. The woman who learned how to stand when it would have been easier to disappear. The woman who learned how to live awake inside her own life.

This is where the story turns outward. You move forward not to prove that healing worked, but because you are ready to live from it. You move forward with your eyes open, your feet grounded, and your voice intact. You move forward knowing that strength and softness can coexist, that clarity does not require certainty, and that becoming is something you embody, not chase.

There may still be days when old patterns try to resurface. There may still be moments when fear whispers familiar lies. But you are not who you were. You have faced what tried to shape you. You have named it. You have surrendered it. And you have chosen differently.

You are not becoming her someday. You are choosing her now. And that choice is powerful enough to shape everything that comes next. You once learned how to brace.

Now you are learning how to breathe.

The wreckage did not define you. It revealed you. Now walk in who you have become.

ABOUT THE AUTHOR

Paulette Boone is a writer, life coach, and encourager who is passionate about helping women rediscover hope, healing, and purpose after life's hardest seasons. Her work is rooted in honesty, compassion, and the belief that even the most broken chapters of our stories can become places where healing begins.

Paulette has been married to her husband, John, for more than three decades. Together they have built a life shaped by faith, perseverance, and the lessons learned through seasons that both tested and strengthened their marriage.

As a mother and Mimi, Paulette understands the beauty of family as well as the quiet weight many women carry while trying to hold everything together. Her life experiences have deepened her empathy for those who feel overwhelmed, unseen, or uncertain about the path ahead.

Through her writing and her coaching, Paulette creates spaces where people can slow down, be honest about their struggles, and begin rebuilding their lives with clarity, courage, and grace.

At the heart of everything she does is a simple belief: no matter how broken the past may feel, healing is possible and hope can rise again.

STAY CONNECTED

Thank you for taking this journey with me.

If the words in this book spoke to your heart, I would love to stay connected with you. My hope is that the conversations we begin in these pages can continue beyond the final chapter. Healing and growth are not meant to happen in isolation, and there is always more encouragement waiting for you along the way.

You can find additional writing, resources, and ways to connect through the spaces below.

Author Website

For updates on future books, reflections, and writing from my personal journey, visit: **www.pagesoflegacy.com**

Pivot Point Life Coaching

Pivot Point is the space where I offer Life Coaching packages. A way to connect with me on a deeper level. I share coaching insights, encouragement, and resources designed to help women rediscover their strength, their purpose, and their faith during life transitions.

Visit: **www.pivotwithpaulette.com**

A FINAL THANK YOU

If this book encouraged you, consider sharing it with someone who may need these words right now. Sometimes a single page can become the beginning of healing for someone else.

And if you would like to support the message of this book, leaving a review where you purchased it helps more readers discover the hope found within these pages. Thank you for reading and for allowing me to walk beside you in this part of your story.

With you in the aftermath, **Paulette**

www.ingramcontent.com/pod-product-compliance
Lightning Source LLC
Chambersburg PA
CBHW021529150726
47990CB00006B/2152